The thaw

A Play

Sylvia Cullen

NEW ISLAND

First published in Ireland in February 2001
by New Island Books, 2 Brookside,
Dundrum Road, Dublin 14

Copyright © 2001 Sylvia Cullen

The right of Sylvia Cullen to be identified as the author of this work has been asserted by her in accordance with the Copyright, Designs and Patents Act, 1988

ISBN 1 902602 50 1

New Island Books receives financial assistance from The Arts Council (An Chomhairle Ealaíon), Dublin, Ireland.

New Island Books gratefully acknowledges the generous assistance of Wicklow County Council towards the publication of this play.

Caution
All rights in this play are strictly reserved and application for performance rights should be made to the Irish Writers Centre, 19 Parnell Square, Dublin 1. No performance may be given unless a licence has been obtained. Requests to reproduce the play in whole or in part should be addressed to the publisher.

This paperback edition is sold subject to the condition that it shall not, by way of trade or otherwise, be lent, resold, hired out, or otherwise circulated in any form of binding or cover other than that in which it is published and without a similar condition, including this condition, being imposed on the subsequent purchaser.

Acknowledgements
Thanks to Leah Coyne and Wicklow County Council, everyone at Tinahely Courthouse Centre and New Island Books, all those who agreed to be interviewed for the research process and everyone involved in both productions.

Printed in Ireland by Colour Books Ltd.

To Terence with love

Author Note

Sylvia Cullen grew up in West Waterford and now lives in County Wicklow. She studied drama at the Samuel Beckett Centre, Trinity College, Dublin, graduating in 1989. Her plays include: *Crows Calling*, Firkin Crane Theatre Cork; *Chrysalis*, City Arts Centre Dublin, Group Theatre Belfast, The Playhouse Derry and Triskel Arts Centre Cork; *Flood*, Project Arts Centre and *Hunting the Strawberry Tree*, which toured national schools in Munster and Leinster. She has scripted two devised shows: *Owl*, Cork City Hall and *Broken Ground*, national tour. A recipient of several Arts Council awards, she was recently appointed Writer-in-Residence at Baltinglass Hospital.

New Island • New Drama: Other Titles in the Series

A Dublin Bloom, Dermot Bolger
April Bright & Blinded by the Light, Dermot Bolger
Greatest Hits: Irish One-Act Plays, Edited by Dermot Bolger
The Passion of Jerome, Dermot Bolger
Rough Magic: First Plays, Edited by Siobhán Bourke
Observatory, Daragh Carville
Ladies and Gentlemen, Emma Donoghue
Class Acts, Clare Dowling and Caroline Williams
A Night in November, Marie Jones
This Lime Tree Bower, Conor McPherson
St Nicholas & The Weir, Conor McPherson
Cell, Paula Meehan
A Radical Guide to Macbeth and Hamlet, Fintan O'Toole
The Politics of Magic: Tom Murphy, Fintan O'Toole
Catalpa, Donal O'Kelly
Judas of the Gallarus, Donal O'Kelly
The Gay Detective, Gerard Stembridge
Long Black Coat, John Waters
The Way You Look Tonight, Niall Williams

The Thaw was commissioned under the Arts Council Arts Centres Commissioning Scheme. It was first performed at the Tinahely Courthouse Centre on 17 November 1999.

Cast:
JOHN-DAN LONERGAN: Noel Dalton
DERRY LONERGAN: John Dolan
MARY-JO LONERGAN: Anne Hickey
PASCAL MOUNSEY: Rory Healy
MIXIE PHELAN: Padraig Darcy
VIOLET GRIMSON: Sue Wardell
SOREN WADE: Pauline Dolan
STACIA FOY: Monica Canna
NEILUS GRIMSON: Dave O'Kelly

Director: Magie Gallagher
Designer: Terry Corcoran
Production Manager: Bree Greene
Stage Manager: Ina Santi
Sound Design: Ian Laidlaw

The production to coincide with this publication was directed by Terence White with the following cast changes:

MARY-JO LONERGAN: Kathleen Nolan
PASCAL MOUNSEY: Jimmy Hennessy
MIXIE PHELAN: Ken Moore
VIOLET GRIMSON: Anita Whitty

CHARACTERS

JOHN-DAN LONERGAN, fifty-four

DERRY LONERGAN, thirty

MARY-JO LONERGAN, sixty

PASCAL MOUNSEY, twenty-nine

MIXIE PHELAN, twenty-one

VIOLET GRIMSON, fifty

SOREN WADE, twenty-eight

STACIA FOY, forty-seven

NEILUS GRIMSON, thirty-five

The play is set in a townland near Tinahely in County Wicklow. The action takes place during the Big Snow of 1947.

SET

There are three doorways in Lonergan's kitchen: a back door leading outside, a door to the parlour and another leading upstairs. As was the custom, each is covered by a heavy curtain. There are two windows in the kitchen.

DRESS

The men wear wooden-soled clogs or boots.

Soren is dressed in mourning and wears a black sealskin coat.

ACT I

Scene One

The evening of February 2nd, 1947. Lonergan's kitchen. A song is playing on the radio. Mary-Jo is standing over Derry who is seated at the table. John-Dan stands by the window, looking worried.

MARY-JO: Hold still! Stop your wriggling!

DERRY: I can't help it, 'tis paining me.

MARY-JO: Derry Lonergan you're worse than any chap.

DERRY: Are you trying to kill me off with that stuff?

MARY-JO: Looka that, he doesn't even trust me!

JOHN-DAN: Ha?

DERRY: 'Course I do.

MARY-JO: Good. Open your gob so.

DERRY: I trust you with my hair, not with my back teeth.

JOHN-DAN: Looka that moon — for God's sake! I knew it all along.

He switches off the radio.

MARY-JO: One more drop and you'll be right.

DERRY: Mary-Jo I'm telling you, my tooth'll cure itself!

She grabs his jaw.

JOHN-DAN: Sheep shoulda been brought in. They'll smother up in them hills.

DERRY: (*Jumping up*) God blast it!

JOHN-DAN: Derry! What did I say about cursing in this house?

MARY-JO: 'Tis the iodine is annoying him. (*To Derry*) Well there's no other cure.

JOHN-DAN: I don't like the looka that sky one bit. And see the way the smoke is blowing back down the chimney?

MARY-JO: (*Picking up a handkerchief off the floor*) Looka this John-Dan, there's gratitude! No more Christmas presents for you, boyo.

DERRY: (*Taking it*) Ah stop, it fell out of my pocket.

MARY-JO: Oh all the hours I spent embroidering that.

DERRY: (*Folding it on the table*) Ohhh!

MARY-JO: And I never once seen you use it.

DERRY: Sure it's far too good to go emptying my nose into.

MARY-JO: (*Smiles*) Can I empty the rest of this iodine into your tooth, or will I send you down to see Stacia?

DERRY: (*Taking up a copy of 'The Wicklow People'*) No!

MARY-JO: (*Putting away the iodine*) God's sake, I'm giving up on you altogether! From this on out, you may go to Stacia Foy for your cures ... John-Dan, come away from the window.

JOHN-DAN: Ha?

MARY-JO: My God tonight, sit down man.

JOHN-DAN: I can't be easy.

MARY-JO: Why not? What's wrong with you?

JOHN-DAN: I'm afraid of my life it's going to snow. That's what.

MARY-JO: Not at all! 'Tis far too cold to snow.

JOHN-DAN: *(Sitting at the table)* Well 'tis looking quare bad outside.

MARY-JO: Ah sure 'tis always bad when you're doing the looking.

JOHN-DAN: *(Preparing his pipe)* The old moon's inside in the new — that's always a bad sign. There'll be no start made on the ploughing now.

DERRY: Stop worrying Daddy, 'tis too early to plough. We won't get going for another while.

JOHN-DAN: You've it all worked out have you?

DERRY: Amn't I the one working it out for the last fifteen year? Don't worry, I'll tell you when it's time to take to the clay.

MARY-JO: *(Smiling)* Your favourite time of year.

DERRY: *(Winking)* Aye, sure there's nothing like it! …

JOHN-DAN: This economic war's a bloody curse so 'tis. Sick to death of it. And no return.

MARY-JO: Oh, I'd hate to be out in that frost. And the wind'd cut you. The boys won't be rambling up this night.

DERRY: Only wait and see! Sure 'tis early yet.

Pause. Mary-Jo takes up her embroidery.

JOHN-DAN: What's the paper news Derry?

DERRY: Little lad from Arklow summonsed and fined. He'd no light on his bicycle.

JOHN-DAN: Read the forecast there, what're they giving for the week?

DERRY: They're giving frost but no snow. *(Reading)* "Black frost blowing in the east wind. Arctic conditions across the whole of Ireland."

MARY-JO: Oh stop! I feel perished with the cold already.

PASCAL: *(Offstage)* Get outa me way!

MIXIE: *(Offstage)* For the love of God!

The boys burst in the back door.

PASCAL: Phelan!

MIXIE: Will you stop trampling me!

MARY-JO: Well, if it isn't the boys themselves.

PASCAL: John-Dan.

MIXIE: Mary-Jo. Well Derry—

PASCAL: How's the tooth?

DERRY: What kept ye — I thought ye must surely be dead.

The boys laugh.

PASCAL: Half-froze alright.

MIXIE: We nearly went skating instead.

JOHN-DAN: Is it snowing yet Pascal?

PASCAL: Snow?

MIXIE: No snow sir. Quare hard frost though.

PASCAL: And heavy skies.

MIXIE: That's the third night of black frost you know.

PASCAL: 'Tis the coldest night the longest I remember.

MIXIE: And Dog Durkan out walking the roads!

They collapse laughing and take off their coats.

DERRY: What's got into Mrs Durkan?

MARY-JO: Where's she walking the roads to at this hour?

MIXIE: Pascal told her one of the Caffertys is dead!

PASCAL: And she's gone up the road like an engine!

MIXIE: To sympathise!

PASCAL: We got her lovely!

DERRY: Oh she'll murder you yet Mixie!

MIXIE: 'Twas he told her not me!

DERRY: She'll hop off of the pair of ye, I know she will!

MARY-JO: These dodges are getting worse Pascal.

PASCAL: Sure if you're not playing jokes you may be dead. That right John-Dan?

JOHN-DAN: Begob mankind, that one deserves it.

PASCAL: Aye, she does.

MIXIE: She does surely.

JOHN-DAN: Whether the Caffertys deserve her in on top of them is another matter!

MARY-JO: *(Standing up and shivering)* Honest to God, I can't keep warm this night. I'm going up to get the jar, beds'll need extra warming. *(Exiting)* Could be there's a window open upstairs.

PASCAL: *(To John-Dan)* You know she's far too good to him don't you? He'll never find a wife!

JOHN-DAN: 'Course he will!

PASCAL: Suppose the land'll attract some woman alright. But he'd want to hurry up, wouldn't he?

DERRY: Speak for yourself Mounsey.

Pascal laughs.

Act One, Scene One

JOHN-DAN: Oh this night reminds me of nineteen and seventeen. Just the very same with the wind howling down the valley.

MIXIE: Are you coming to the dance in Shillelagh?

DERRY: Tonight?

MIXIE: Whole parish is going.

JOHN-DAN: Not this night Mixie.

PASCAL: Why? Didn't he work hard enough?

JOHN-DAN: We're going to have snow! I'm certain sure of it.

DERRY: We'll go down as far as the mill in a while. See is there any stir going on.

Mixie hogs the fire. Pascal joins the two Lonergans at the table and Derry turns to him.

DERRY: Name of God, will you look at the size of your man's clogs! Are they new?

MIXIE: What d'you mean the size of them? They're ordinary size.

DERRY: Sure God almighty man. *(Digging Pascal)* Wouldn't you say they're quare big-looking?

PASCAL: Well true as God now, they're not small. I'll tell you that much Mixie.

MIXIE: Not small how are you — my two feet are the daintiest here!

Derry and Pascal cheer.

PASCAL: Looka that for rashness!

DERRY: The daintiest? Would you say?

MIXIE: Let ye all remove your clogs and stockings. Then we'll see!

DERRY: Stop acting the cod — you're not serious!

JOHN-DAN: Come on now Derry, you started it. He's only finishing.

Reluctantly, Derry and Pascal remove their footwear and stockings. They place their naked feet up on the table.

PASCAL: Well damn you Derry Lonergan, for all this foolishness!

DERRY: I was meaning the new clogs — not the size of his blooming feet!

MIXIE: New clogs — sure they're me brother's. But now we're going to find out. Now we'll see who's the tidiest pair of feet.

JOHN-DAN: My God Pascal Mounsey — the dirt!

PASCAL: Sure what's wrong with you — that's clean dirt.

JOHN-DAN: I'll allow you've never bothered with them, not since the nurse washed them!

PASCAL: D'you hear him talking!

JOHN-DAN: *(Placing his naked feet on the table)* D'you ever use a drop of water?

PASCAL: I do 'course. Now and again. Same as yourself by all accounts.

DERRY: Only once a month by the looks of it.

PASCAL: Once a month? Once a year'd do me!

Pascal grabs the handkerchief to give his feet a wipe.

DERRY: Gimme that here!

PASCAL: What?

DERRY: You're not using this to wipe your mucky toes!

PASCAL: Jakers, 'tis only a hanky Derry.

JOHN-DAN: Mixie Phelan — the potatoes you're growing in there!

MIXIE: And what about yourself sir? I can see mangolds and parsnips on your soles!

PASCAL: Derry's growing oats in beside his two big toes!

DERRY: Well you've your own bloody turf bank there!

MIXIE: Aye begobs, but 'tis I has the daintiest feet.

JOHN-DAN: *(Cleaning his toes)* True for you Mixie, aye.

PASCAL: You never uttered a truer word.

Dogs bark outside. Mary-Jo returns.

MARY-JO: Boys-the-man, what now! What kinda exposure is this going on!

DERRY: We're having a 'daintiest feet' competition.

MIXIE: *(Wriggling his toes)* And I'm the champion.

JOHN-DAN: Fair dues!

MARY-JO: A disgrace the whole lot of ye!

PASCAL: Mary-Jo have you a scissors handy? I've an awful desire to cut me nails.

Suddenly the back door bursts open and Violet Grimson struggles in from the wind. She looks at the men in confusion. Everyone stares at her as she retreats slightly.

VIOLET: I shoulda knocked — I did mean to knock.

MARY-JO: No harm Missus, stay where you are. *(To the men)* Dress ye'reselves for God's sake! Missus stand up to the fire there, recover yourself.

VIOLET: No I can't, I — It's my niece, she's —

MARY-JO: Yeh?

VIOLET: She's outside.

DERRY: Is there an accident?

JOHN-DAN: Give her a chance will you!

MARY-JO: Whist up! Missus speak.

VIOLET: My niece and I, we ... we were travelling but we can't continue, it's freezing!

JOHN-DAN: 'Tis no night for a journey Missus.

VIOLET: No ... So we were wondering, if ... if at all possible — we have to have shelter for the night!

JOHN-DAN: Shelter, she says.

MARY-JO: Of course Missus—

VIOLET: Just for the one night, that's all. I promise.

MARY-JO: Derry will you give the poor woman that chair!

JOHN-DAN: Sit down, take your ease.

VIOLET: No you see, my niece, she's—

MARY-JO: She's outside yet?

JOHN-DAN: I'll bring her in.

VIOLET: No wait! First I, I have to tell you, she, she's ... Well she's, in a certain condition.

JOHN-DAN: A certain, condition you say?

VIOLET: Yes. Very much so ... *(Looking at Mary-Jo)* A delicate condition.

DERRY: What, is she diseased?

MIXIE: Rheumatic fever! A lad died of it only last week near Hacketstown!

VIOLET: No! Not sick, incapacitated. She's … *(Appealing to Mary-Jo)* She's with —

MARY-JO: Oh! I get you! I get you now Missus of course!

PASCAL: Shove round there Derry for God's sake!

DERRY: Go easy.

VIOLET: You don't mind? Just for the one night?

MARY-JO: Go out and get her for the love of God. Bring her in!

VIOLET: Oh thank you. Thank you!

She exits. Pause.

JOHN-DAN: Outsiders Mary-Jo. You didn't even ask their name!

MARY-JO: Will you whist up — sure what could we do?

JOHN-DAN: They're not from this country — total strangers!

MARY-JO: For one night John-Dan. The poor woman nearly out of her wits! …

JOHN-DAN: Go out you two — not you Derry! Stable the horses and carry in whatever belongings they have.

PASCAL: Come on Mixie.

MIXIE: You go first!

They exit.

DERRY: I'm going as well—

JOHN-DAN: You'll do what you're told! Sure you'll be better able to talk to them.

MARY-JO: Cover up your naked feet Derry! ...

JOHN-DAN: *(To Mary-Jo)* Don't you go offering the last of the tea now d'you hear? We're low enough on provisions ... They can do with a drop of milk, or cocoa.

MARY-JO: *(Going to the door)* Come on in here Missus, come and heat ye'reselves by the fire!

Soren enters supported by Violet. She is six months pregnant.

DERRY: Here, here's a chair.

VIOLET: She'll be fine now, won't you?

SOREN: Yes. *(To Derry)* Thank you.

Silence.

VIOLET: *(To John-Dan)* I am Miss Violet Grimson ... And this is my niece, Mrs Soren Wade.

SOREN: Where are we? *(To Derry)* Are we anywhere near Gorey?

DERRY: Well no, not really. Gorey's a long ways off.

SOREN: Oh.

Pause. Mary-Jo digs John-Dan.

JOHN-DAN: *(To Violet)* This is, this is my son, Derry.

DERRY: *(Shaking hands)* Miss Grimson. *(Shaking hands)* Mrs Wade.

SOREN: *(Smiling)* Soren.

Silence. Mary-Jo clears her throat.

JOHN-DAN: Oh — and this is my sister, Mary-Jo.

VIOLET: *(Shaking hands)* Thank you so much for taking us in.

SOREN: *(Shaking hands)* Pleased to meet you Mary-Jo ...

MARY-JO: And this of course is John-Dan Lonergan, the man of the house.

VIOLET: Mr Lonergan, we're frightfully grateful—

JOHN-DAN: Oh now, John-Dan'll do me!

SOREN: Thank you for this kindness John-Dan. It's arctic conditions outside.

MARY-JO: Arctic isn't the word!

Pause. The boys return.

PASCAL: Horses and car and all's brought in.

JOHN-DAN: Good lad Pascal, thanks ... They won't be frost-bit in the stable anyhow ...

MIXIE: *(Holding two small cases)* Sir — what'll I do with these?

MARY-JO: Out into the parlour with them Mixie. *(To Violet)* We'll fix up some kind of bedding for ye there.

VIOLET: Please, don't go to any trouble on our account.

MARY-JO: No trouble, don't be talkin'!

Pause.

JOHN-DAN: Where's your country Miss Grimson? ...

VIOLET: Oh, we came from—

SOREN: We came across from, the other side of Tinahely.

JOHN-DAN: I see ... I don't know that far country very well myself.

DERRY: I do know a bit of it. I know some of it anyway.

JOHN-DAN: Sure how would you know that country?

DERRY: When you sent me that way, for the threshings. *(To Soren)* Week at a time I was in it. Enjoyed every minute.

Silence. Mixie returns.

MARY-JO: Oh you haven't met the boys yet Miss Grimson. This is Mixie Phelan. Lives with his mother only down the road. Snags all our turnips and fills our potato pit too, don't you Mixie?

JOHN-DAN: And possesses the daintiest pair of feet in all Leinster!

Soren and Violet look at John-Dan and one another.

MARY-JO: And this here's another neighbour, Pascal Mounsey. We're very great with all the Mounseys. And Pascal's the best in the whole townland with a spade. He's a miller at pick and shovel work.

JOHN-DAN: And great at the dodges too, aren't you Pascal?

PASCAL: Oh now, I'm saying nothing! …

JOHN-DAN: Oh aye indeed, we can't complain about the neighbours in these parts. Look at Caffertys. And Huttons. There's two families'd never see you stuck …

PASCAL: C'mon Phelan, are you right? We'll ramble down to the mill.

MIXIE: Are you coming Derry? …

DERRY: Nah, I won't bother tonight.

PASCAL: You said you were coming earlier.

DERRY: No sure, I'll leave it now. I'll go down with ye tomorrow.

PASCAL: Change your mind, did you? *(Smirks)* C'mon Mixie, we'll head.

MARY-JO: Goodnight now boys. We'll see ye tomorrow, with the help of God.

Pause. John-Dan turns to Violet.

JOHN-DAN: It was Gorey ye were headed for, was it?

VIOLET: *(Hesitates)* Well, —

SOREN: No. *(Looking at Violet)* We were, on our way to Dublin.

DERRY: Dublin!

MARY-JO: Sacred!

JOHN-DAN: Not tonight surely?

VIOLET: No, 'course not …

SOREN: Aughrim. We were going to stop in Aughrim.

VIOLET: Yes …

MARY-JO: And what has ye hitting for Dublin in this weather?

SOREN: It's, my sister-in-law. She's in a bad way.

MARY-JO: Oh no.

SOREN: We're hoping to get there, in time.

JOHN-DAN: I see. *(Pause. Looking at Mary-Jo)* I'll be going out to give the beasts their feeding. I'll say goodnight to ye ladies.

VIOLET: Goodnight Mr Loner — Goodnight John-Dan.

SOREN: 'Night …

MARY-JO: *(Pushing Derry out)* You go on out now and help your father while I fix up these ladies. *(Reluctantly, Derry exits. Pause)* Well, 'tis grand to have a bit of female company for a change. My brother's wife died young you see, thirty year ago now, Lord have mercy on her soul … Right, well I'll just, check on the parlour for ye. See what way we'll arrange things.

She exits. Pause.

VIOLET: What sister-in-law?

SOREN: Sssh!

VIOLET: Why on earth did you say Dublin?

SOREN: We can't tell people the truth!

VIOLET: I don't see why not.

SOREN: Neilus'll be furious when he discovers. He's bound to come after us.

VIOLET: Lord almighty Soren, don't be so anxious.

SOREN: But is he catches up with us —

VIOLET: Sssh! Be quiet … Don't worry, we'll be gone out of here at first light tomorrow.

SOREN: We'll have to be, or — (*Holding her stomach*) Oh!

VIOLET: Are you alright?

SOREN: (*Nods*) Just a kick. My poor ribs.

Mary-Jo returns.

MARY-JO: Now ladies, who's for a nice hot bowl of rabbit soup?

Black out. The wind begins to howl.

Scene Two

Three days later. Afternoon of February 5th. A song plays on the radio. Soren is standing by one of the windows, looking out. Derry comes in the back door carrying two buckets of water. He and Soren look at one another, then look away ...

SOREN: You were able to get water?

DERRY: Aye — had to break the ice mind you.

SOREN: Again?

DERRY: *(Setting down the buckets)* 'Tis viciously cold. Well was frozen a good couple of inches. *(He fills two cups)* Here, will you have some?

They drink. Pause.

SOREN: I didn't mean to offend your father yesterday. Asking to milk — I was only trying to help.

DERRY: Sure I know, don't mind him. He was just, worried you might strain yourself. *(Pause)* When it stops snowing, I could bring you 'round a bit. Show you the yard anyway!

SOREN: *(Smiling)* Alright. If it does stop.

DERRY: Aye, still no sign. *(Mary-Jo enters)* I'll head on or the oul' lad'll be after me!

He exits. Mary-Jo turns off the radio.

MARY-JO: We better be saving the battery — you don't mind?

SOREN: No, 'course.

MARY-JO: If this blizzard's going to keep up. Three full days of it, imagine.

SOREN: I've never seen this much snow in my life.

MARY-JO: Such drifts!

SOREN: And still frozen.

MARY-JO: I hope we won't be in for another three days of the same.

SOREN: You don't think so do you? We'll never get away! Get out, I mean.

MARY-JO: Don't be worrying yourself. Sure it's all in God's hands ... Why don't you sit down for a while Soren? You've been watching out that window the whole day.

SOREN: I will. In a while.

Pause. Mary-Jo takes out her embroidery and sits at the table.

MARY-JO: Your husband, you don't mind me asking, was he, how did he die?

SOREN: He was killed in an accident. Thrown off of his horse last September.

MARY-JO: Oh I'm sorry ... Musta been terrible—

SOREN: *(Pacing)* I really hate being stuck inside like this. I have to be out, I need to be. Not used to this at all.

MARY-JO: Sure none of us is ...

SOREN: I do all the milking at home you know. My record is seven minutes per cow.

MARY-JO: *(Laughs)* You could win the All-Ireland, if they had one for milkers!

SOREN: *(Smiles)* I miss it. *(Sitting at the table)* Miss the cows as well.

MARY-JO: Sure you'll be able to go home soon.

SOREN: Aye ...

MARY-JO: Have you names for all of them you have? *(Soren nods)* C'mere and I'll tell you a secret so, I've names on all my hens.

SOREN: Have you?

MARY-JO: 'Course! They're all called after film stars. Gloria, Shirley and Lilian. Greta, Ginger — and the cock's called Fred. *(Both laugh. Pause)* I was just like you, you know, couldn't be kept inside. Couldn't wait to be off to any kind of a dance ... We cycled as far as Craanford sometimes. And the men you'd meet — sacred!

SOREN: What were they like?

MARY-JO: Some of them were right melodeons! I'll allow they could manage the dancing though, I'd have to give them that. *(Smiles)* Those were days ... *(Suddenly Violet screams in the parlour)* Mother of God! *(Violet runs in, shaking)* What happened you?

SOREN: Is someone there?

MARY-JO: Speak!

VIOLET: There was a face!

MARY-JO: Where?

VIOLET: Unnatural, staring in the window she was!

MARY-JO: A woman?

VIOLET: Yes — oh a fright to God.

MARY-JO: That'll be Stacia Foy.

SOREN: Who?

MARY-JO: *(Going into the parlour)* The cure woman. Lives on the edge of the townsland.

VIOLET: Jesus God!

SOREN: Sssh!

VIOLET: My heart!

SOREN: Calm down. You're safe.

VIOLET: The hair on her. And those eyes!

MARY-JO: *(Returning)* Must be gone again. No sign of her.

VIOLET: How can she get around in all the snow?

MARY-JO: *(Shrugs)* That's Stacia for you. Never know where she'll turn up next.

VIOLET: Blast her anyway, frightening me like that. Damn fool! *(Soren digs her)* Oh — I am sorry, I didn't mean to use language.

MARY-JO: Happens to the very best of us Miss Grimson. Sit you down, go on.

VIOLET: I couldn't know what was at the window! And I'm not usually a gibber.

Soren goes over to a window. Mary-Jo hands Violet a cup.

MARY-JO: Here, have a sup of milk.

VIOLET: Thank you Mary-Jo.

MARY-JO: No bother.

VIOLET: Honestly!

Pause. Mary-Jo resumes her embroidery.

MARY-JO: One good thing about this blizzard — 'twill give me a chance to finish off my cloth.

VIOLET: Yes, I'm amazed to see you at that.

MARY-JO: How d'you mean?

VIOLET: Well I didn't think you people did embroidery.

MARY-JO: *(Stopping)* What?

VIOLET: I'd've thought you all, you know, stuck to knitting. Goodness knows why — you're obviously very capable.

26 Act One, Scene Two

MARY-JO: *(Standing and shoving it into her hands)* Maybe you'd be so good as to finish it off for me so.

Mary-Jo grabs the brush and starts sweeping. Soren glares at Violet. Pause.

SOREN: *(To Mary-Jo)* John-Dan and Derry are gone ages. Will I look out and see if they're alright?

MARY-JO: Well it can't be easy dragging hay across the yard in that kinda wind. But I'm sure they'll manage. Same as other people.

Silence.

VIOLET: Soren, honestly!

SOREN: What?

VIOLET: Sit down and brush your hair, can't you. You're making me nervous, keeping watch like that.

Soren sits and starts brushing her hair. Mary-Jo enjoys Violet's struggle with the embroidery.

MARY-JO: *(Coming over beside Soren)* I'd hair like yours once and Mother used brush it for me. Every night, without fail.

SOREN: Mine never bothered. Don't think she'd care if it all fell out.

VIOLET: Soren! That's enough …

John-Dan and Derry come in the back door, taking off layers of clothing once inside.

JOHN-DAN: Oh there's lovely heat!

DERRY: Let me in, quick. That's a sore wind!

JOHN-DAN: Such a snow!

SOREN: Did ye think of checking the road?

DERRY: The road?

SOREN: Yes — is it any way passable?

JOHN-DAN: Sure you wouldn't even be able to make out the road.

DERRY: The ditches are half-covered! You should see it Mary-Jo.

JOHN-DAN: Drifting worse than ever so 'tis. Worse nor thirty-three I'd say. Nor nineteen and seventeen even!

DERRY: It's like magic, the whole townsland's disappeared! Nothing to be seen for miles, only a blanket of white.

Soren and Violet exchange a look.

JOHN-DAN: A most violent snowstorm! Take your breath clean away. You'd need a mask outside to do the simplest of jobs.

DERRY: You would surely — we were nearly smothered.

JOHN-DAN: Looks like ye're here for the long haul alright.

VIOLET: How long?

JOHN-DAN: *(Shrugs)* Well—

SOREN: You must have some idea.

JOHN-DAN: Could be another few weeks I suppose.

VIOLET: *(Standing)* What! Never!

JOHN-DAN: No! I'm only rogueing! Still and all, we could be in for another week at least.

DERRY: We may get used to it alright. *(Glancing at Soren)* Sure it could be worse.

JOHN-DAN: *(Taking out a pack of cards)* Aye …

VIOLET: Well we mustn't lose heart. It can't last forever.

SOREN: No, 'course not ...

MARY-JO: *(To Soren)* You're worried about your family, and your sister-in-law, aren't you?

VIOLET: Yes. But I'm more concerned about putting up here. Imposing on you like this.

JOHN-DAN: *(Shuffling the cards)* Could always go down to Huttons if ye prefer. Then ye'd be imposing on ye're own kind ...

DERRY: Daddy! Name of God, —

MARY-JO: What kinda nonsense are you spouting John-Dan! We'll be alright, even if it does last another week. We'll manage away fine.

DERRY: Aye, 'course we will ...

VIOLET: Look, why don't you take some of our ration coupons. *(Offering her some)* We'd prefer to pay our way.

MARY-JO: Thank you, but no.

VIOLET: Please.

MARY-JO: *No*, I said ... Seeing as we've no hope of getting into Tinahely, they wouldn't be much use to us, would they?

Pause.

SOREN: *(To Derry)* Your hair's soaking — you'd want to dry it.

DERRY: Nah — I'll be fine!

MARY-JO: Thinks he's immune! *(Handing Soren a towel)* You do it for him will you? *(To Derry)* One of these days you'll catch pneumonia!

Soren hesitates but does. Pause.

JOHN-DAN: We may all turn in early tonight. Save on firewood, in case it does last the week.

DERRY: Sure Will Hutton's only after offering us fuel. *(To Mary-Jo)* Imagine he struggled over to check were we alright.

MARY-JO: He's a decent man is William Hutton. Great neighbour. Couldn't best him.

DERRY: He was amazed when I told him about our unexpected guests!

Soren looks at Violet.

VIOLET: Yes but, like I said, as soon as ever the roads are clear, we'll be going.

SOREN: That's if the snow ever stops … We're well and truly stuck you know.

MARY-JO: You'll see, the rain'll be along soon. Then ye can make ye're escape!

SOREN: Escape? What d'you mean?

MARY-JO: I'm only joking you!

SOREN: Oh …

JOHN-DAN: Well, who's for 'nother game?

He smiles around at them all. Black out.

Scene Three

A week later. Night of February 12th. Soren is pacing the kitchen by the light of the Sacred Heart. She stops over by a window and feels her stomach, sighs.

VIOLET: *(Entering from the parlour)* Lord above Soren, what're you at? *(Soren starts laughing at her)* What do you find so amusing?

SOREN: Your hair, it's wild!

VIOLET: Sssh! And why wouldn't it be? I'm tossing and turning all night because of you.

SOREN: That's why I came out here.

VIOLET: *(Peering at her reflection)* If anyone saw me, I'm like a walking sceach! ... C'mon lady, back inside to your bed.

SOREN: It's no use.

VIOLET: Come on!

SOREN: But I can't sleep!

VIOLET: Quiet! ... May as well keep you company so. *(She lights up a Woodbine)* Only eight left. Oh well, one a day I suppose.

SOREN: Isn't it just like sleeping inside in a chapel. That statue of the Virgin — I keep thinking she's going to speak!

VIOLET: You're alright, you only have Mary. I'm stuck in between Saint Anthony and the Child of Prague!

Both laugh. Pause.

SOREN: It's just so strange to be here. I can't get used to it.

VIOLET: I know this past week's been hard—

SOREN: It feels like gaol! And when's it going to end?

VIOLET: Just count your blessings, we were very lucky they took us in.

SOREN: I know. *(Pause)* Look, I meant to say to you, I really appreciate what you did.

VIOLET: Nonsense!

SOREN: No, honestly—

VIOLET: Sssh! ...

SOREN: If you hadn't helped me, —

VIOLET: I only did what I felt was right. Couldn't stand by and, pretend. That was all.

SOREN: But Violet—

VIOLET: Now we're not going to dwell on it. I insist ... What about Mary-Jo — wouldn't she talk the teeth off a saw!

Both laugh.

SOREN: John-Dan's a gas oul' member isn't he? Lives on cards!

VIOLET: If he asks me to play another game of Old Maid! ... At least I got a chance to have a go at the cooking today. I don't mind fried rabbit ordinarily, but not three blinking days in a row! *(Pause. A horse whinnies and Soren jumps)* Poor horses are restless too. They're not used to no exercise for days on end ... *(Violet puts her arm around Soren)* You'll have to stop worrying about Neilus you know, put him right out of your head. D'you hear me?

SOREN: I can't help it, I was never fonda him. You wouldn't know what he might do.

VIOLET: No one can travel anywhere in this depth of snow. So it's pointless fretting ... It'll only take us two days to get from here to Rosslare. Once we're on that boat, we'll be safe. Alright? *(Soren nods)* Now come on in to your bed soon. Don't leave me on my own with all these saintly men!

She exits to the parlour. Silence. Soren goes over to the window, holds back the tears, unsuccessfully. The door to the stairs opens and Derry shuffles in, wearing long johns and holding a candle. After a moment he sees Soren and stops dead, shocked. They stare at one another.

DERRY: I, I didn't know anyone was here. Just came down for a sup of milk ... Had a wicked pain in my stomach after Violet's boiled onions. *(Soren smiles and wipes her face)* What's wrong?

SOREN: *(Turning away)* Nothing. I just wasn't able to sleep.

DERRY: *(Going towards her)* Were you crying?

SOREN: Sssh! Someone'll hear. *(Moving away)* I just, just couldn't get to sleep. It's so silent ...

DERRY: Aye, I know what you mean. Amazing how the heaviest snowfall can change everything without making a sound. *(Going nearer)* You were crying, I know you were.

SOREN: It's nothing ...

DERRY: Is it your husband, you're missing him still?

SOREN: No! I'd be missing him if he'd ever felt like a husband. But he never did, always working. Always walking away he was ...

DERRY: What is it then? You can tell me.

SOREN: I can't!

DERRY: Trust me Soren. *(He takes her hand)* I could never walk away from you.

Pause.

SOREN: If I tell you, will you promise not to say anything?

DERRY: I swear.

SOREN: You won't breathe a word?

DERRY: I won't tell a soul. *(Pause. She squeezes his hand)* There isn't any sister-in-law, is there?

SOREN: No ... This all started last summer — you remember the dreadful rain?

DERRY: Never forget it.

SOREN: Well our harvest was disastrous, the whole crop was lost. We were facing ruination — complete disaster ... Then, after my husband was killed in the accident, my father changed. He just ... Well, he was different.

DERRY: Why?

SOREN: He was desperate, he knew things were looking hopeless.

DERRY: So what happened?

SOREN: I'm just, I'm coming on it now. *(She glances at the parlour door)* My first cousin, Neilus Grimson's his name ...

DERRY: Go on.

SOREN: He came to my parents with a plan — and they just seized on it!

DERRY: What sorta plan? ...

SOREN: They want to force me to marry Neilus.

DERRY: What!

SOREN: My father says it's the only way to save the farm.

DERRY: God almighty what kinda, tyrant is he?

SOREN: That's why me and Violet fled — we had to escape before the baby is born. She's been great. Only for her I'd never've got out.

DERRY: So where were you running away to, that night?

SOREN: Rosslare. To get the boat to England. I just had to get out!

DERRY: It's alright ...

SOREN: Neilus is only doing this for the land — and the moneya 'course!

DERRY: You're safe from him now, don't worry.

She kisses him. Suddenly there's a sound from the parlour.

VIOLET: *(Offstage)* Soren — what're you doing?

SOREN: Quick! Hide!

Derry dives under the table. Soren blows out the candle.

VIOLET: *(Entering)* What's going on? Were you talking to someone?

SOREN: Yes. I was ... To the baby.

VIOLET: Lord almighty, the child can't hear you Soren. But everyone else in the place will. Now get into bed, at once!

Soren exits followed by Violet. After a moment, Derry comes out and smiles to himself. Sneaking over to the stairs door he knocks against a bucket.

DERRY: Agh, Jesus!

He freezes, holding his foot with one hand and the bucket with the other. He listens for a moment, waiting for a reaction, then rushes out.

Scene Four

A week later. Mid-afternoon on February 19th. Lights up on Mary-Jo sitting at the table, peeling potatoes. Derry paces from one window to another, glancing at the parlour door and staring out at the snow.

MARY-JO: Poor John-Dan …

DERRY: What? What did you say?

MARY-JO: Your father.

DERRY: What about him?

MARY-JO: Finding the two dead beasts this morning, dealt him an awful blow … Doesn't suit him to be kept from the stock like this.

DERRY: Doesn't suit me either — what can we do?

Mary-Jo looks at him.

MARY-JO: What's got into you Derry Lonergan? You're like two tigers, the whole of this past week.

DERRY: What're you talking about?

MARY-JO: Look at you!

DERRY: I'm fine.

MARY-JO: All distracted.

DERRY: I'm not, just — Leave me be, will you.

MARY-JO: Only trying to help. Don't like to see you distressed.

DERRY: Mary-Jo I'm not in the least bit distressed! *(Pause. Violet comes in the back door)* How're the horses? Alright?

VIOLET: Poor things, they could do with a right good gallop. They won't know what's hit them when we're on the move again! *(Derry turns away. Pause)* Anything I can do Mary-Jo? Let me give you a hand with some of the potatoes.

MARY-JO: No, not at all, won't take me a minute.

VIOLET: You're sure now?

MARY-JO: Aye … I noticed you left a few bits of peel on the ones you did Sunday.

VIOLET: Did I?

MARY-JO: Here and there just.

VIOLET: Really? …

MARY-JO: 'Course you mightn't be used to being as particular as what we are.

VIOLET: I see. *(Pause. She takes out her cigarettes)* Lord save us, only one left! Oh well, may as well enjoy my last one. *(Pause)* Oh, I meant to say to you … I'm afraid I'd an awful, accident last night …

MARY-JO: What kinda accident?

VIOLET: In the parlour, with Saint Anthony.

MARY-JO: The holy water font, is it?

VIOLET: No no, the man himself.

MARY-JO: *(To Derry)* Sacred she's after breaking Saint Anthony. Knew I shoulda taken them all out. I said damage'd be done!

VIOLET: No he's not broken, just chipped … It's his necklace really.

MARY-JO: His rosary you mean.

VIOLET: Yes …

MARY-JO: I'll bring them all up to my own room later.

VIOLET: Would you mind? That'd be marvellous. It's a bit crowded when you're groping 'round in the dark. *(Silence)* You're very quiet today Derry. You've hardly said a word.

MARY-JO: Oh I'm very worried about him. You're not yourself sure you're not?

VIOLET: Maybe you need more rest?

MARY-JO: Is it your tooth at you again?

DERRY: No. I'm fine ... Just wasn't bargaining on another week stuck inside.

MARY-JO: Sure where d'you want to be going?

DERRY: Ah, nowhere.

MARY-JO: Thinks he's missing out.

DERRY: Well I am! May be sure of it.

Silence. John-Dan enters from the stairs door. He sits and starts cleaning his pipe.

JOHN-DAN: I'm awful worried 'bout the ewes Derry. We'll have to go up after them.

DERRY: 'Tis pointless Daddy! Not until the snows ease off.

JOHN-DAN: Caffertys'll help. I know they will.

DERRY: What we need is a decent dog.

JOHN-DAN: What?

DERRY: You shoulda got a better dog, I told you!

JOHN-DAN: You'll get your chance Derry. Can get all the dogs you like.

DERRY: Sooner the better.

JOHN-DAN: I'll allow you'll keep your imperence to yourself!

Silence. Soren enters from the parlour. She and Derry exchange a glance.

VIOLET: *(To John-Dan)* A few of the horses shoes are getting a bit rusty.

JOHN-DAN: So? ...

VIOLET: Well, I—

JOHN-DAN: You think I didn't notice?

Soren takes the brush and starts sweeping.

VIOLET: Well I was only pointing it out in case—

JOHN-DAN: There's nothing can be done 'til there's some let up. Whenever that'll be.

MARY-JO: Whenever God decides ...

PASCAL: *(Offstage)* Lonergans, hello!

MIXIE: *(Offstage)* Anyone home?

The back door bursts open and in sweep the boys.

PASCAL: Derry are you there?

MIXIE: The boys is back!

MARY-JO: A miracle! Boys — come in let ye.

DERRY: How did ye get here?

MIXIE: Walked the ditches!

PASCAL: How d'you think?

JOHN-DAN: Well fair dues!

MIXIE: Couldn't see any landmarks at all. The drifts are that high!

PASCAL: And frozen solid. Hard as rock!

MIXIE: Did ye ever see snowstorms like them?

PASCAL: Barbarous. Barbarous!

JOHN-DAN: True for you.

MARY-JO: We haven't seen anyone for weeks.

MIXIE: Sure no one has. Except for Stacia Foy.

JOHN-DAN: A hardy lady, ha? You wouldn't want to cross Stacia.

MIXIE: She must be stirring the pot quare fast this weather!

MARY-JO: Oh boys, ye remember the strangers don't ye? Well, not really—

DERRY: Not strangers now, surely.

MARY-JO: No, 'course not.

Pause.

JOHN-DAN: What's the news of the townsland anyhow?

MARY-JO: Anybody dead?

MIXIE: Nah. All cooped up like pigs in a pen.

PASCAL: Not a stir. All stuck indoors.

MIXIE: Everybody waiting for the thaw.

DERRY: Like ourselves …

VIOLET: *(To Pascal)* So no improvement at all then?

PASCAL: Worse it's getting! Supposed to be nine inches of frost down Carnew way yesterday.

MARY-JO: No!

PASCAL: True as God — it's after killing off anything there was in the ground.

JOHN-DAN: My God there'll be no ploughing done. No planting at all.

PASCAL: And the drifts!

MIXIE: Mountains of snow!

SOREN: It's unbelievable.

MIXIE: 'Tis supposed to be up over the telegraph wires in Tinahely.

MARY-JO: Go 'way!

DERRY: Are you serious?

JOHN-DAN: Be the hokey man, ha!

PASCAL: Sure we were able to walk out of Mixie's below and up on top of a drift so high, we were looking down Dog Durkan's chimney!

MARY-JO: Sacred! Boys! She'd eat ye if she knew.

PASCAL: People are venturing out a bit today though.

MIXIE: Aye begobs.

PASCAL: No horses mind, only on foot! 'Twill be a while before anyone'll make an attempt to hit into Tinahely.

MARY-JO: Boys-the-man, I hope 'twon't be too long. We could do with stocking up on supplies.

JOHN-DAN: We may clear out the town altogether!

DERRY: Sardines — and corned beef!

VIOLET: A packet of Woodbines!

SOREN: Some chocolate!

DERRY: Didn't know you were fonda chocolate …

JOHN-DAN: I'da thought, Miss Grimson, you'd've other things on your mind, if and when you do manage to reach Tinahely.

VIOLET: Other things?

JOHN-DAN: 'Course! ...

VIOLET: What kinda things John-Dan?

JOHN-DAN: Notifying the guards.

SOREN: The guards!

VIOLET: About what?

JOHN-DAN: So they'll inform ye're relations ... That ye're safe!

VIOLET: Oh!

JOHN-DAN: *(Looking at Mary-Jo)* And they'll come and get ye!

VIOLET: Well, yes. 'Course.

MARY-JO: *(To Soren)* And your sister-in-law, you'd like word of her, wouldn't you?

SOREN: Yes, I would alright.

Silence.

PASCAL: *(To John-Dan)* I'm told there was a sighting of another outsider person. Last week, over Kilquiggan way.

Soren looks at Violet.

JOHN-DAN: A stranger?

PASCAL: Aye, a man. So I'm told anyway ...

Derry glances at Soren.

VIOLET: Whereabouts was he supposed to be going, this stranger?

Pascal shrugs.

MIXIE: Headed for Tinahely, wasn't he?

PASCAL: Imagine it, out in them snows!

JOHN-DAN: Begob mankind, he's either a very foolish or a very desperate man!

Soren suddenly sinks into a chair. Derry rushes over to her.

DERRY: Soren are you alright!

MARY-JO: What happened her?

VIOLET: *(Pushing Derry out of the way)* Look at me.

JOHN-DAN: Is she after fainting?

SOREN: I'm just dizzy.

DERRY: *(Pushing back in)* Will I get a drink of something?

MARY-JO: Leave her Derry, let the poor woman get her breath.

VIOLET: Soren, come on outside a minute.

SOREN: I'm alright now, really.

VIOLET: *(Pulling her up)* You need to get a bit of air, that's what's wrong. C'mon out with me, now!

Soren exits supported by Violet.

DERRY: Looka what you're after doing Mounsey!

PASCAL: What did I do — it wasn't me.

DERRY: Big gom!

MARY-JO: Whist up!

PASCAL: If the cat has kittens 'round here 'tis I'm blamed!

DERRY: You're some gobshite! …

PASCAL: *(Winking at Mixie)* If I near fainted I bet he wouldn't go running to get a drink!

Mixie and Pascal collapse laughing.

DERRY: Shut your mouth you, you hoor!

MARY-JO: Derry!

JOHN-DAN: Leave it so!

MARY-JO: Stop all that unpleasantness now! No fights.

Pause. John-Dan pulls on his coat.

JOHN-DAN: *(To Derry)* C'mon you — before the sun goes and sets on us.

DERRY: What now?

JOHN-DAN: The blasted hoggets, that's what! They need their fodder, the little we have to give 'em.

Derry pulls on his coat and hat.

PASCAL: We'll go with you John-Dan.

JOHN-DAN: No need. We'll manage away fine. Mind ye'reselves on them ditches boys. Don't go doing ye'reselves any injuries!

He and Derry exit. Mary-Jo collapses onto a chair.

MARY-JO: Outa the house I thought they'd never go!

MIXIE: John-Dan is it, and Derry?

MARY-JO: No!

PASCAL: The other two, fool!

MARY-JO: The women, aye.

MIXIE: Oh.

MARY-JO: Such a time! I never put in the like of it, in the whole of my life. I'm absolutely jaded!

MIXIE: Why?

MARY-JO: They've been here over a fortnight and the place was like a session house! Hardly nobody speaking only myself.

PASCAL: *(Winking at Mixie)* Go 'way!

MARY-JO: I never saw four such awkward people.

MIXIE: Well ye're stuck with them now. They can't go anywhere 'til it stops drifting.

MARY-JO: I know — and John-Dan's resenting every mouthful they eat.

MIXIE: Quare lively though, aren't they?

MARY-JO: Hm! I never set eyes on two such wound-up women.

PASCAL: Excitable are they?

MARY-JO: Always on edge. Always watchful. I'm not able for much more of it, I'm telling ye ... As for Derry, sacred, I don't know what's got into him. A right strange humour he's in ...

Pascal gestures at Mixie.

MIXIE: Mary-Jo? Any chance of ...

MARY-JO: What? Will you speak up!

MIXIE: Any chance of a spare egg?

MARY-JO: An egg! And me with two women to feed on top of ourselves!

PASCAL: Ah go on, give us an oul' egg!

MIXIE: I've nothing ate since yesterday.

PASCAL: Oh the angry little sizzle and it hitting the hot bacon fat!

MIXIE: Mother used always give me a bottle of milk with a raw egg whipped in and the tiniest spoon of sugar.

They sigh in ecstasy and glance at Mary-Jo.

MARY-JO: The one egg between yous so. *(The boys whoop and cheer)* Only don't say I gave it you, d'you hear me now?

MIXIE: A boilt egg — all runny!

PASCAL: No fried!

MIXIE: I said boilt!

PASCAL: Fried! You little poultice! *(Mixie hits Pascal a box that sends him flying to the ground)* What the curse in hell! What did you strike me for, you bog-eel!

MARY-JO: Boys will ye quit!

MIXIE: You dirty-looking oul' yawn!

PASCAL: *(Getting up)* C'mon so you little yellow lump!

MIXIE: *(Backing away and banging into Mary-Jo)* Mounsey you crooked oul' divil!

MARY-JO: Ow! Janey!

PASCAL: C'mere to me you Phelan!

MARY-JO: *(Grabbing the brush)* Out! I'll flake ye! *(Hitting them)* Get out this minute!

PASCAL: Aagh!

MIXIE: Stop! Mary-Jo!

PASCAL: Are you trying to kill us?

MARY-JO: Outa my sight the two of ye!

Mary-Jo lunges and chases them out the back door.

PASCAL: Mind me legs!

MIXIE: God in heaven—

PASCAL: Get her away from me!

MIXIE: Have mercy!

The boys yelp as the lights fade.

Scene Five

Two weeks later. The morning of March 5th. Lights up on Soren and Derry in the kitchen. A song plays on the radio. Soren's left hand is wrapped in Derry's handkerchief.

DERRY: *(Whispering)* I was trying to talk to you last night!

SOREN: But didn't you see? Violet was watching ...

DERRY: If only we could go out!

SOREN: I was awake the whole night, most of it anyway. Listening to Violet snore!

DERRY: If I snore — would you still love me?

SOREN: Well ... You may sleep with a flour bag over your head.

DERRY: *(Going to kiss her)* I may never sleep again.

SOREN: Are you sure your father's gone out?

DERRY: Yes! Definitely.

Just as he goes to kiss her, Mary-Jo enters from the stairs door. Derry moves away and Soren sits down.

MARY-JO: Found the jumper anyway.

DERRY: Did you? Great ...

MARY-JO: My God tonight the cold!

She begins darning the elbow of a jumper. Pause.

DERRY: *(To Soren)* How's your hand feel now?

SOREN: *(Shrugs)* Just the same.

DERRY: Still sore?

SOREN: Yes, very. I can't believe I was so careless.

MARY-JO: Lucky 'twasn't your whole arm ...

Act One, Scene Five

DERRY: You should bathe it in cold water again.

SOREN: I told you already—

MARY-JO: Will you ever stop at her! Isn't he worse than a clocking hen? *(Violet comes in the back door)* Leave her be can't you, declare to God!

DERRY: Sorry.

SOREN: It's alright.

DERRY: Only trying to help … What the blazes is keeping her anyway? She said she'd folly me directly.

MARY-JO: Sure she's to get through all the snow and ice.

VIOLET: She should never've been sent for in the first place! …

MARY-JO: Excuse me Violet, are you addressing that remark to me?

VIOLET: Who else?

MARY-JO: Well I'll have you know it was Derry who went off and—

VIOLET: I'll allow he went but I'm sure you sent him!

MARY-JO: Indeed and I did not! He took off by himself. It was his own idea entirely! …

VIOLET: Well I'm, sorry then. I do apologise.

MARY-JO: Hm! …

VIOLET: *(To Derry)* I really wish you hada consulted me first.

DERRY: Sure how could I, you weren't here!

VIOLET: Lord God! I was only feeding the horses.

SOREN: Violet, there's no need to cause a tieration! We just panicked when it happened.

VIOLET: *(To Soren)* Well I wish you'd had the wit to come to me … Doesn't look too bad, we coulda—

SOREN: It's quare painful. It was boiling water!

VIOLET: Righto, fine! …You know we'll be on the road soon enough. We can easily call to a doctor then, if you're still mewling and complaining.

SOREN: If you got scalded you might complain too!

VIOLET: Not for a thing of nothing I wouldn't!

Soren looks at Derry.

MARY-JO: I like the way you're so confident about being able to travel soon. They're giving it bad again you know.

SOREN: Surely not. It lasted all February, it can't last the whole of March into the bargain.

Silence.

VIOLET: I'm really not happy about this. Not happy at all.

MARY-JO: *(Laughing)* Just because she gave you a bit of a fright.

VIOLET: It's not that.

MARY-JO: Look if there's one good thing about Stacia Foy, she does know her cures.

DERRY: Aye, she does.

MARY-JO: I'd have to give her that much anyway.

VIOLET: Well you wouldn't think it to look at her!

DERRY: Sssh! …Thought I heard her voice.

Silence.

MARY-JO: *(To Derry)* C'mere what're you waiting 'round for anyway? …

DERRY: Why shouldn't I wait?

MARY-JO: And your father needing help? Can't you see you're only making poor Soren nervous.

DERRY: I'll be going out to help him in a minute. *(Soren gestures to him to go)* Soon as Stacia arrives, I'll go.

Pause.

VIOLET: *(To Mary-Jo)* D'you want more firewood brought in or anything?

MARY-JO: No, don't dream of troubling yourself.

VIOLET: Wouldn't be any trouble.

MARY-JO: Well we've plenty, thanks …

Suddenly Stacia opens the back door and enters. Everybody stands and turns to look. Silence as she stares around at them.

STACIA: Am I at the right house at all? Ye look as if ye were expecting a ghost. Or worse …

MARY-JO: Come in Stacia. Come on in of course …

DERRY: This is Soren. The woman I told you hurt her hand.

SOREN: Hello … Pleased to meet you.

DERRY: And this here's her aunt, Miss Violet Grimson.

Violet nods and Stacia stares at her. Neither one moves.

MARY-JO: You'll have a sup of something before you start … We've cocoa. Or milk … We're, we're outa tea with all the rations—

STACIA: Nothing. Don't want anything … I'm here outa curiosity really. *(To Soren)* Don't usually cure many of your kind …

VIOLET: You may find there's not that much to be cured.

MARY-JO: Well now—

DERRY: I wouldn't say that, Violet.

SOREN: I was badly scalded.

MARY-JO: She hasn't been herself this past fortnight so she hasn't. Not since the night the boys were here.

STACIA: And what's gone wrong?

MARY-JO: She's all pale and fretful.

SOREN: *(Smiling)* That's not true!

MARY-JO: Not sleeping right either.

SOREN: Mary-Jo I don't think you—

MARY-JO: And she's no appetite!

VIOLET: *(To Soren)* Happy now?

SOREN: *(To Stacia)* Look it's just the burn, honestly.

STACIA: Tell me so — how did it come about?

SOREN: Well, I was—

DERRY: It was an accident! Boiling water spilled out on her from the pot.

SOREN: Yes — I picked it up too quickly.

VIOLET: It was overfilled if you ask me.

MARY-JO: No 'twasn't!

VIOLET: Dangerously overfilled!

Mary-Jo glares at Violet who looks away.

STACIA: *(To Soren)* I see you're nearing your confinement.

Violet looks at Stacia in horror. Derry doesn't know where to look.

SOREN: Oh yes. I am …

STACIA: Hoping for a boy or a girl?

SOREN: Well, either. Either one'll do me fine …

MARY-JO: It's really only her hand Stacia—

STACIA: I'm fully aware of that …

She squats down beside Soren and starts taking off the handkerchief. Violet moves in closer.

MARY-JO: *(Whispering to Derry)* My God tonight! You may go out to John-Dan!

DERRY: I told you, I'm going! Will now, in a minute.

Pause. Stacia holds up Derry's handkerchief.

STACIA: This yours?

DERRY: Yeh 'tis. *(Looks at Mary-Jo)* Couldn't help it, was the first thing I laid hands on.

MARY-JO: No matter …

STACIA: Looks sore enough.

SOREN: *(Looking away)* Feels red raw so it does. Can you do anything to ease it?

STACIA: Well … *(Soren grimaces as Stacia makes her close and open her hand)* You're in for a rough oul' time of it, dying skin and blood blisters.

VIOLET: Whatever you're thinking of putting on it, I want to know first.

Pause. Stacia stands and looks at Violet, then Derry.

STACIA: I think you may find someone else to do your curing. This Miss doesn't like the looka me. I can feel it from her.

DERRY: But it's Soren needs the cure.

STACIA: Looka her standing in on topa me! *(Violet moves back slightly)* Breathing her fumes down me neck! Doesn't trust me nor me cures, I can tell. Ye only like ye're own kind to treat ye, that right? Protestant swine!

SOREN: What!

Soren looks at Derry.

DERRY: Stacia Foy you get outa here right now!

STACIA: You've no sway to go putting me out. This is your father's house.

Derry flings her bag at her and shoves her violently towards the back door.

MARY-JO: Derry!

DERRY: Get out to blazes, I mean it!

MARY-JO: No, don't! …

STACIA: I came here to give help and that's the thanks I get, putting me out!

MARY-JO: No Stacia, he didn't mean it! …

STACIA: You'll have no luck for this Derry Lonergan!

Slowly she turns and goes. Terrible silence.

MARY-JO: What've you done?

DERRY: *(To Soren)* Are you alright? … Well are you!

SOREN: Yes …

MARY-JO: What're you after bringing on us Derry?

DERRY: You heard what she said. I had to—

MARY-JO: You'd no right throwing her out! No right in the world.

DERRY: She went too far Mary-Jo.

MARY-JO: There are other ways, besides doing that ... My God, what'll John-Dan say? Nobody tell him a word!

DERRY: *(Grabbing his coat)* I'm going outa this. I'm getting out!

He bangs out the door.

SOREN: No Derry, wait!

VIOLET: *(Pulling her back)* Come back here you outa the cold!

MARY-JO: I'm going out after him. *(Pulling on her coat)* He never acts like this!

She runs out the door.

VIOLET: Have you lost your reason?

SOREN: Let go of me.

VIOLET: Let her worry about him—

SOREN: *(Breaking away)* Violet will you leave me be!

Violet stares at her.

VIOLET: Sooner the better you have this baby, before you bring—

SOREN: It's not the baby, it's—

VIOLET: What then?

SOREN: It's— *(Turning away)* just the snow, smothering everything! *(Going to a window)* Look at it there, spitting down again!

The lights fade as the wind rises.

Scene Six

A week later, March 12th. A bright moonlit night. A barn owl calls out as the lights reveal a snow-covered ditch on Lonergan's land.

PASCAL: *(Offstage)* Hold up Phelan! Will you wait!

MIXIE: *(Offstage)* C'mon if you're coming. Catch up!

Mixie enters, followed by Pascal.

PASCAL: Jakers, what's the big rush?

MIXIE: Nothing.

PASCAL: Well you coulda fooled me!

MIXIE: It's too bloody cold to be mooching 'round. Shagging snow! Sick to the back teeth of it … Soon be Patrick's Day — how long more are we going to have this hardship?

PASCAL: *(Blowing on his hands)* Couldn't tell you. Even the weathermen don't know.

Suddenly Mixie freezes.

MIXIE: *(Whispering)* What the divil was that? Did you hear something?

Pause.

PASCAL: Quit your rogueing!

MIXIE: I heard a sound!

PASCAL: *(Stamping his feet)* There's nothing there.

MIXIE: Looka the hairs gone out through my cap! … The lads're on Lonergan's lane I'll bet. Kicking football up along … Oh be the tarlin' mankind the lads loves this snow.

PASCAL: Well they'll have more of it tomorrow, going by that moon. Looka her up there, going down on her back.

They stare up. Pause.

MIXIE: Arra c'mon into Lonergans Pascal, it's icy standing here!

PASCAL: You may forget about Lonergans as long as them two women are holed-up inside in it. Ruining everything with their manners and their modes!

MIXIE: *(Kicking at the snow)* What're we doing here so? That's all's I want to know.

Pause.

PASCAL: Begod I could eat a roomful now!

MIXIE: I tell you!

PASCAL: The hunger's fierce.

MIXIE: A penny loaf, with treacle on top.

PASCAL: Oh stop!

MIXIE: I'd go to hell for one of 'em!

PASCAL: Or a mess of salted herrings.

MIXIE: Aye!

PASCAL: Gor I'd walk to Arklow to taste them.

MIXIE: You would surely. So'd I.

Pause.

PASCAL: Never thought Cafferty'd refuse John-Dan a bit of help finding the sheep.

MIXIE: The divil fire on that crowd anyway!

PASCAL: But he shoulda known the kinda them.

MIXIE: Everyone else is dirt in the rye!

PASCAL: And when you thinka him and Derry, last summer in all the wet? Killing themselves for Cafferty.

MIXIE: Aye.

PASCAL: Reaping and binding his corn after the deluge. Barbarous. Barbarous!

They sigh. Pause.

MIXIE: Jays you shouldn'ta started on food there Pascal. Talking of herrings has my tongue crying out for a plateful.

Suddenly Stacia appears, carrying a bundle of sticks. Silently, she walks up beside the boys.

PASCAL: What about a slice of bacon?

MIXIE: Go 'way!

PASCAL: Or a juicy rabbit, boilt and fried.

MIXIE: Stop! You're tormenting me.

STACIA: Well boys.

MIXIE: Janey God!

PASCAL: Bloody hell! Stacia!

MIXIE: My heart!

STACIA: Ah now boys, calm ye'reselves.

MIXIE: Merciful hour!

PASCAL: Where did you spring outa?

STACIA: No snow'll repress me. I came out to cut a few sceachs.

MIXIE: Oh jay I wouldn't touch them Stacia — the lads don't like it.

STACIA: Arra what lads! No such thing! Can't beat a sceach for firing Mixie. As good as coal — better even! … What news of Lonergans these days — still harbouring the two women?

PASCAL: Aye, seem to be alright ...

STACIA: Where did them two come in from anyhow?

MIXIE: *(Shrugs)* Couldn't rightly say. Haven't got a clue as a matter of fact! ...

STACIA: *(To Pascal)* And what were they doing on the road? ... Mounsey I'm asking you a question!

PASCAL: *(Moving away)* Sure what're you looking to me for, I wouldn't know the first thing about 'em.

MIXIE: John-Dan you'd have to ask. Or Derry.

PASCAL: What're you so interested for anyhow? ...

STACIA: 'Tis kinda unusual isn't it though? Two women out journeying at night, alone.

MIXIE: Aye begobs, 'tis. And plenty bags and belongings with 'em.

Pascal gesticulates at Mixie.

STACIA: Bags. Had they bags? Good man Mixie Phelan.

PASCAL: *(To Mixie)* C'mon you. We'll hack up to my sister, said she'll give us a feeda something.

MIXIE: Did she? Oh thanks be to God!

PASCAL: We'll see you Stacia.

STACIA: Are ye away?

PASCAL: Aye. Me stomach is weak with the hunger.

STACIA: Go on so, wouldn't like to see you expire.

PASCAL: Goodnight now.

MIXIE: 'Night Stacia.

They exit. Pause. A barn owl calls out. Stacia turns to go but stops and squints down the fields. She hesitates, then hides in behind the ditch. *After a moment, Soren and Derry enter; Soren's hand is still bandaged.*

DERRY: That's settled then?

SOREN: Yes. Kiss me again so.

He does.

DERRY: Just a small wedding. No big fuss — right?

SOREN: With a real good hooley after the breakfast, everyone up dancing! I'll be well able for foxtrotting by then.

DERRY: You can teach me so.

SOREN: Derry, *(Putting his hand on her stomach)* you're sure you don't mind about …

DERRY: I told you — 'course not!

SOREN: And you'll treat the child the same, as any others?

DERRY: Yes. I promise you …How soon is it going to be?

SOREN: Only about, 'nother six weeks. *(Smiling)* I don't want to think about it yet though …

DERRY: There hasn't been a child born at home since myself … *(Hugs her)* I can't believe it you know. I feel so lucky! And you'll love it here, you'll see.

SOREN: Aye, must be heaven in the summer.

DERRY: A real paradise so 'tis … And the land is generous here. Not the besta land maybe, but giving at the same time … We'll not be discontented here Soren, I'm sure of that.

Pause.

SOREN: How're we going to tell them though? I'm not certain how Violet'll take it.

DERRY: I may speak to John-Dan first. Prepare him slowly.

SOREN: Violet might insult him you know. Sometimes she'll pass a remark and say such a one married beneath herself. I hope she won't make a row.

DERRY: Don't worry, Mary-Jo won't let her.

SOREN: *(Nods)* I shouldn't speak bad about her — only for her I wouldn't be here!

DERRY: Show me your poor hand. Is it nearly better?

SOREN: Not yet — sure it's only been a week. *(She kisses him)* Another thing Derry, I'm thinking I should tell John-Dan and Mary-Jo the truth. Explain the real reason why we were travelling.

DERRY: Well look, let's sit tight 'nother little while. It's not the best time to go telling anything, when we're all snowed in together …

SOREN: *(Shivers)* I better get back you know. Violet'll miss me.

DERRY: Aye, Mary-Jo'll think I'm drifted.

SOREN: Don't let on so — whatever you do!

DERRY: *(Nods)* I won't pretend anything. *(She kisses him)* You're frozen.

SOREN: I don't care!

DERRY: Well I do — now go on in. I'll folly after. I'm going up the fields first. And mind yourself — keep to the ditches.

SOREN: I will!

Derry exits. Silence. The barn owl calls again. Soren looks around, sensing something. She backs away slowly and exits. Stacia emerges, triumphant.

STACIA: Now Derry Lonergan, ha? Putting me out like a dog! ... Well I'll bring your hooring to a halt so I will. I'll pitch it right out into the open!

She raises a stick and violently breaks it in two. Black out.

ACT TWO

Scene One

March 15th. John-Dan and Derry are standing on the side of a hill as the sun is starting to set. They hold long poles for finding sheep and are staring into a hollow. An arctic wind blows from the east.

JOHN-DAN: I'm wondering how long it takes a sheep to smother. A week? A day? Few hours?

DERRY: God only knows Daddy. God only knows …

JOHN-DAN: Ours didn't deserve this burial so they didn't! What way're we going to be fixed now? *(Derry shakes his head)* Quare big loss — to go replacing alla them?

DERRY: We will replace them.

JOHN-DAN: How?

DERRY: I don't know but we'll do something! … We're not letting this finish us. We'll survive it someway.

Pause.

JOHN-DAN: If we'd only brought them in you know. If we'd caught them before that last snowstorm.

DERRY: But sure we tried, you know we did.

JOHN-DAN: If them bastards of Caffertys hada helped — God blast them! If they'd given us a few hours, this coulda been prevented!

DERRY: 'Course it could.

JOHN-DAN: There's a neighbourly act for you ha!

DERRY: They're just not worth it, that crowd.

JOHN-DAN: Whole flock wiped out. If I coulda saved one even!

DERRY: How many others are saying the same thing—

JOHN-DAN: I only care about mine! Damn the bit of me gives a curse about the rest ... All in lamb, every one of 'em. A fortnight from yeaning ... To smother like that under the snow, it's ... *(Shouting)* What the hell're you trying to do to us?

DERRY: Daddy!

JOHN-DAN: You think we'll go under? We'll not!

DERRY: Leave it will you!

John-Dan shrugs Derry off. Silence.

JOHN-DAN: If your mother was here, she'd be saying a prayer for the sheep. *(Smiles)* Just the same as if a person had died ... She was always living from the heart, your mother ... *(Turning away)* Great pity she was called before you'd a chance to —

Silence. Derry makes a move towards him but goes over instead to the hollow and marks the spot with his pole.

DERRY: *(Softly)* We'll have to come back up for them another time Daddy. After Patrick's Day.

JOHN-DAN: Is it Patrick's Day tomorrow?

DERRY: The day after. *(He looks along the horizon)* C'mon, this light's not going to last.

JOHN-DAN: I know. You'd better be getting back. Pascal and Mixie could be off making snowmen! The last of them potatoes has to be got in from the pit today.

DERRY: I'll look after it, don't be worrying yourself. I'll make sure it's done.

JOHN-DAN: *(Turning to him)* Your mother'd be quare proud son. You're going to make a grand joba this place, I know it ... *(Derry smiles)* Thank God for it often. I do! Gives me great peace, knowing the land'll go to you. In time, when you've, settled down and all.

DERRY: *(Looking away)* Aye.

JOHN-DAN: And I know you will. Someday. You're a careful chooser but 'twill come. God'll send you a wife, don't worry.

John-Dan blows his nose. Derry glances over at him. Pause.

DERRY: Violet's idea 'bout the frost nails was a good one, wasn't it?

JOHN-DAN: *(Sighing)* Aye, the woman knows her horses alright.

DERRY: And Soren does too — she spotted that flesh-wound before any of the rest of us. If the dandruff hada got into that ...

JOHN-DAN: I don't know how we're meant to keep on feeding them two women. Supposed to stay the one night, here they are — more'n six weeks!

DERRY: Sure where could they go? You couldn't put them out into this. *(John-Dan blows on his hands and rubs them)* You talk to Soren easy enough now, don't you?

JOHN-DAN: Sure she's grand to talk to. But fitful. Something uneasy 'bout her, as if she's holding back the whole time.

Pause. Derry moves nearer.

DERRY: Daddy, —

JOHN-DAN: Looka that now — more spitsa snow! Whole valley still covered, 'tis unnatural.

DERRY: Look, I was going to say to you—

JOHN-DAN: Serve oul' Cafferty right if his roof falls in — d'you see the slate gone?

DERRY: Yeh I do. Listen, Daddy—

JOHN-DAN: What's wrong? Is something wrong?

Derry looks at him then looks away.

DERRY: I was going to, to say to you.

JOHN-DAN: What — we've no mangels left? Well God blast, I knew it!

DERRY: No! You're not listening.

JOHN-DAN: What is it then, the bullocks?

DERRY: It's nothing got to do with the bullocks! … There was something I wanted to— … Ah nothing!

JOHN-DAN: Can't you tell me?

DERRY: *(Looks away)* Not now, 'nother time. Have to get back to the boys.

He walks off.

JOHN-DAN: Derry, wait!

DERRY: I'll see you below at the house!

He exits. John-Dan looks after him, puzzled, squinting into the twilight. Stacia appears and approaches slowly. She carries two dead rabbits.

JOHN-DAN: Missus Foy.

STACIA: Mister Lonergan … 'Nother most violent snowstorm, wasn't it though?

JOHN-DAN: Blinding altogether …

STACIA: Hitting the whole district mighty hard.

Stacia goes to pass on but John-Dan prevents her.

JOHN-DAN: What did I warn you about snaring rabbits on my land?

STACIA: *(Smirks)* Wasn't on your land I got these.

JOHN-DAN: Where then?

STACIA: Below in Caffertys. *(John-Dan backs off)* They wouldn't see a neighbour starve, God bless 'em! *(Pause. John-Dan turns away)* You never came for your cure Mister Lonergan.

JOHN-DAN: Cure for what? I'm not wanting any cure from you.

STACIA: Chillblains wasn't it?

JOHN-DAN: *(Laughs)* Sure where's the harm in them.

STACIA: Been saving my waters for months for you.

JOHN-DAN: Wasting your time Stacia — go back to watering the clay!

STACIA: One good soaka your feet and I'll have you cured forever more!

JOHN-DAN: Begob mankind, I'll not be soaking my toes in your waters! *(Both laugh)* I'd sooner take a knife and cut my feet off altogether! ...

STACIA: *(Indicating the hollow)* How'll you replace your losses?

JOHN-DAN: Sure there's no replacing losses. They're gone now and that's it.

John-Dan starts walking away.

STACIA: Oh, Mister Lonergan.

JOHN-DAN: *(Stopping)* What the hell d'you want now! *(Turning on her)* You're always looking for something.

They stare at one another until John-Dan looks away.

STACIA: Ah, maybe 'tis as well left alone. You'll find out yourself, in time.

She turns away. He shivers.

JOHN-DAN: *(Impatiently)* What d'you mean? What'll I find out?

She turns and looks at him, starts stroking one of the rabbits. Slowly the twilight turns to dusk.

STACIA: *(In a low voice)* Someone's fooling you Mister Lonergan. Been feeding you a packa lies.

JOHN-DAN: What's that? What did you say?

STACIA: Lies. *Lies* I'm saying. You're after being deceived.

JOHN-DAN: By who? Is it Cafferty?

STACIA: *(Shakes her head)* 'Tis them two women you brought into your home. You let 'em come in didn't you?

JOHN-DAN: *(Hesitating)* I did, aye! ... They just, come along in the night.

STACIA: *(Smirks)* God help you — is that what you were told? And you believed them, did you?

She laughs in his face. He retreats.

JOHN-DAN: Listen here Stacia I've work to get done. Go on outa this, find someone else to listen to your blather!

STACIA: *(Going towards him)* Them two've been lying since the night they arrived.

He sniffs and looks away.

JOHN-DAN: What would you know 'bout them two anyway?

STACIA: I'll tell you what I know — they're keeping something from you! Don't want you rooting out the truth.

JOHN-DAN: *(Laughs)* Where did you get this nonsense? Go on and don't be causing trouble!

STACIA: I heard 'em myself. Saying they'll have to keep the truth from you! And not only that ... *(Stroking the other* *rabbit)* I'm sorry for you Mister Lonergan, I am. You're after bringing poison into your own home.

JOHN-DAN: Poison. *(Suspiciously)* What're you saying?

STACIA: Them women couldn'ta turned up by chance you know. They musta come to you deliberate, they're after something alright.

JOHN-DAN: After what?

STACIA: *(Shrugs)* Sure what're any of them crowd after the whole time? *(She glances at him. Pause)* Your son's mixed in with it as well you know.

JOHN-DAN: Derry?

STACIA: I wouldn't fool you when it comes to your own son.

JOHN-DAN: What about him? ... If you know something say it!

STACIA: He's hiding things, keeping his goings-on from you.

JOHN-DAN: What goings-on?

STACIA: *(Sneering)* Suppose they suit one 'nother really.

JOHN-DAN: *(Turning her towards him)* Who?

STACIA: The widow woman ... *(John-Dan freezes)* She's after gorging his heart with notionsa love, fattening him up like a pig. And now it's too late. *(Clutching him)* She's got him to promise he'll marry her!

JOHN-DAN: *(Pushing her off)* My Derry! Going marrying her?

STACIA: Aye — sure that's all he wants now, whether you like it or not. He's in thrall to her, he won't listen to reason.

JOHN-DAN: *(Turning away)* No, I don't believe a word of it.

STACIA: *(Catching his arm)* They lied to you, all of them, even your own son! *(Facing him round)* If you don't believe me go down and ask him. Ask him now yourself! Show him 'tis you hold the reins of the house!

Stacia exits quickly. Dusk has given in to night. John-Dan clutches his pole, motionless. He holds himself back until he's certain Stacia is gone.

JOHN-DAN: He'll listen alright, may be sure he will ... Go marrying her — is that what he thinks? *(Pause. His face darkens)* No, I'll not tolerate it! No Protestant's coming in on my land ... Cursed bloody grabbers — *never*!

Black out.

Scene Two

Later that evening. The lights come up on the kitchen where Pascal and Violet, Mary-Jo and Mixie are twirling at the tail end of a wild dance. Soren cheers and claps them — her hand is no longer bandaged.

MARY-JO: Boys-the-man Violet, I never thought you had it in you!

VIOLET: Oh it's in me alright, don't you worry!

MIXIE: Oh jay, my poor legs. My arms are broke!

MARY-JO: Let's have another one, c'mon boys!

PASCAL: *(Groaning and turning off the radio)* Oh jakers, no!

VIOLET: Not straightaway? I couldn't!

MARY-JO: Who's for the Berlin Polka — Pascal!

PASCAL: Are you codding me Mary-Jo?

MARY-JO: Sailor's Hornpipe so. *(Grabbing him)* Mixie are you right?

MIXIE: *(Escaping)* No! Are you trying to kill me!

SOREN: *(To Violet)* Never knew you were so good on your feet.

VIOLET: Hm! Neither did I.

MARY-JO: Ah, I haven't danced like that in years.

VIOLET: *(Going towards a comb chair)* I'll have to sit down, I'm winded.

MIXIE: Not there! *(Violet starts)* Not in that chair Missus …

VIOLET: Why not? I've been sitting on it inside in the parlour for weeks. *(Looking at Mary-Jo)* Is there something wrong with it?

PASCAL: That's the lying chair.

MARY-JO: So 'tis, I forgot!

PASCAL: Don't ye have liars corners in ye're country?

MIXIE: Whoever sits in that has licence to tell nothing but lies all night!

PASCAL: Stuff the chicken with lies, that right Mixie?

SOREN: Let me have it so.

She sits in it.

PASCAL: Oh now, an upstanding widow like yourself wouldn't tell any lies. *(To Violet)* Would she?

SOREN: *(Grins)* You might be surprised Pascal.

VIOLET: *(Sharply)* Soren!

The boys look at one another.

MARY-JO: *(Sighs)* Thought this night was going to be lively.

SOREN: *(Claps)* Yes, dead right Mary-Jo!

VIOLET: For heaven's sake go easy! You'll have to go into bed soon. *(Soren folds her arms)* You need your rest!

SOREN: Rest! Sure we're only getting going!

MARY-JO: C'mon Mixie, you'll start us off on an oul' story.

PASCAL: That's it Mary-Jo — Phelan for a story!

SOREN: Go on, Derry says you're a dickens for telling stories!

MARY-JO: He's a miller!

MIXIE: *(To Mary-Jo)* Will I tell the one about the flitch of bacon follying the tramp?

PASCAL: No! I'm sick and sore of hearing that one.

MARY-JO: Why don't you give us the one about the little lads — and the horse breaking out in a white sweat!

MIXIE: Arra you've heard that one umpteen times.

PASCAL: *(Whispering)* Tell us about that night you were took.

MIXIE: When I couldn't get outa the raheen?

PASCAL: Aye!

MIXIE: Nah, I'd nearly be afraid speaking of that.

MARY-JO: And there's me thinking you were a bravo. Bragging in the daytime and won't say nothing when the dark is on!

VIOLET: Maybe it's just as well. Must be getting very late—

MIXIE: Here, I have one, I have one!

PASCAL: Listen, sssh!

SOREN: Great! Go on Mixie …

Violet glares at Soren.

MIXIE: I was only a chap at the time, sheltering outa the rain below in Cafferty's barn. The like of the rain you never saw!

PASCAL: Go on, forget about the rain!

MIXIE: 'Twas at the edge of dark this happened and I always had a fear in the dark. Next thing anyways, I hears this breathing. Big, deep, forceful kinda breath. Now I always imagined I was tough, but straightaway I fell on my two knees, couldn't think nor speak! Aye begobs, and what did I see flashing out before me, coming toward me in the depth of the night?

VIOLET: Oh Lord! What was it?

MIXIE: Barbarous big bacon knife — jays a lad about that length! Begod I thought to myself, I'm going outa this! But ne'er the two legs'd stir. Sure I thought I was dead. I'd to check my poor heart and see if it was still going. Next thing, I looks up! And bearing down, right on top of me—

Derry bangs open the back door and some of the firewood he's carrying drops. Everyone jumps.

MARY-JO: Sacred!

VIOLET: Oh dear Lord save us!

PASCAL: Good man there Derry, you're after making the whole room jump!

SOREN: *(Smiling)* Mixie has us all on edge here.

DERRY: *(Putting down the sticks)* Good lad Mixie Phelan!

MIXIE: I wasn't finished you know!

DERRY: *(To Mary-Jo)* Is Daddy not back yet?

MARY-JO: No, I don't know what could be keeping him. C'mon now Pascal, your turn. Give us an oul' song or something.

DERRY: Aye do — give us a blast of the hat? Go on!

PASCAL: The hat is it?

DERRY: Aye!

MIXIE: Aye begobs!

MARY-JO: Oh *The Tinahely Hat*, c'mon Pascal!

PASCAL: Well sure, I'll do me best.

Derry and Mixie whoop and cheer.

MARY-JO: Whist up, here 'tis! *(To Pascal)* You start off and we'll all join in on the chorus.

74 *Act Two, Scene Two*

Pascal takes the floor, prepares himself and sings:

PASCAL:
'It's sold in Weirs and Symes and in shops around the town.
And worn on great occasions with style and renown.
It features in Coolattin and in Killaveney too,
But it's brand is 'Tinahely', a local through and through.

The Tinahely Hat, me boys, it now is all the go.
The Coolboy boys have got it and the boys around Coolroe.
And from there to Aughavannagh, it is worn by one and all,
The boys from Knockananna wear no other hat at all.'

(Loud cheers and shouts from everyone except Violet)

'When Parnell came to Boleybawn he asked about its fame.
And a woman said "Here's a hat that'll surely make your name."
He took it very proudly and placed it on his head.
And the woman said "Now Charles, you are a thoroughbred!" '

As they sing the final chorus, John-Dan comes in the back door, takes off his hat and coat. Clapping and loud cheers from everyone except Violet as they finish.

JOHN-DAN: What the blazes is going on in here? Are ye trying to wake the whole parish? ...

DERRY: We're only having a bit of a song.

JOHN-DAN: Well that's the last song this night. *(To Mary-Jo)* Surprised at you! D'you want the priest in on top of us?

MARY-JO: But sure—

JOHN-DAN: Still Lent you know! Or are you after forgetting your faith?

DERRY: Can't you leave us be—

JOHN-DAN: *(Banging the table)* You'll do what you're told Derry! ...

MIXIE: Sorry for upsetting you sir.

PASCAL: Didn't mean any harm.

JOHN-DAN: Get the hell outa this, the pair of ye!

MARY-JO: John-Dan, what're you at? What's happened?

The boys scuttle out. Silence. John-Dan glares at Soren and Violet.

JOHN-DAN: *(Going towards Soren)* I see you found the lying chair at last. Bare-faced liars the pair of ye. *(To Violet)* Sit down you!

SOREN: *(Standing up)* John-Dan leave her alone.

JOHN-DAN: I don't take orders from the likes of you. Liars and deceivers — and God knows what else!

DERRY: You've no right to go terrorising people like that!

JOHN-DAN: That's the last imperence I want outa you! I won't be lied to in my own house — by anyone.

MARY-JO: Who's after upsetting you?

JOHN-DAN: Never mind who! *(To Soren)* I want to know what's been going on for the last six weeks.

VIOLET: This was all a mistake, we didn't mean to deceive anyone.

JOHN-DAN: I'll be the judge of that — after I hear what she has to say.

VIOLET: Tell him Soren. It was the blizzard! We had to find shelter—

SOREN: I promise you, we thought we'd be gone, the very next morning.

JOHN-DAN: You expect me to believe ye came in here by pure chance?

Soren looks at Violet.

VIOLET: Go on, you may tell him everything ...

SOREN: The night you took us in, we were after fleeing, going on the run.

MARY-JO: On the run?

SOREN: Yes.

MARY-JO: *(Looks over at John-Dan)* Running from who?

SOREN: From my homeplace. My parents, well my father really. *(To John-Dan)* See he's after getting into terrible financial trouble—

JOHN-DAN: I don't give a God-damn 'bout your father!

DERRY: If you're not letting her speak, 'tis pointless—

JOHN-DAN: What were the pair of ye coming in here for — I want answers!

SOREN: But I'm explaining!

VIOLET: She's trying to tell you!

MARY-JO: *(Going to John-Dan)* Calm yourself! Will you not leave the poor woman talk?

JOHN-DAN: Poor woman! Are you blind — or just quare stupid!

Mary-Jo moves back from him. Pause.

SOREN: Look, the truth is, the reason I left, my father wants to force me to get married. To Neilus Grimson, my first cousin, Neilus Grimson.

MARY-JO: Force you?

DERRY: *(To John-Dan)* D'you hear that?

SOREN: He says I've no choice John-Dan, the man won't listen to reason.

VIOLET: No, he won't. Never has in his whole life!

SOREN: He allows it's the only way to keep the land in the family, as well as keeping the name with it.

VIOLET: And he's adamant, absolutely set!

MARY-JO: My God.

SOREN: The night we stopped here, we were trying to get to Rosslare.

VIOLET: I thought we could catch the boat to England but, well — you know the rest.

DERRY: *(To John-Dan)* D'you see? D'you understand now?

SOREN: We only lied because we were afraid to trust anyone. Neilus is bound to come after us.

JOHN-DAN: Is he?

VIOLET: Yes, he's not the kind to give up easy.

Pause. Derry watches John-Dan.

DERRY: What? What is it? ...

JOHN-DAN: There's someone seen a stranger over Coolattin way yesterday.

DERRY: Yesterday?

SOREN: That's him. *(To Violet)* It can only be Neilus.

JOHN-DAN: So I'm told anyway ...

SOREN: Then he is giving chase. *(Looking at Derry)* I knew he would.

Pause. John-Dan looks from her to Derry.

JOHN-DAN: And what're you keeping so quiet for?

DERRY: *(Looks away)* No reason …

JOHN-DAN: You don't look one bit surprised to me. You knew 'bout this didn't you? … Answer me damn you!

MARY-JO: John-Dan there's no need—

DERRY: Alright! I did know. Now — are you satisfied?

JOHN-DAN: And how come you knew before the rest of us?

DERRY: *(Shaking his head)* Daddy just, leave it.

JOHN-DAN: How the hell is it you knew already? I'm asking you Derry!

DERRY: Because Soren told me everything. *(Violet looks from Derry to Soren)* She told me the whole story.

JOHN-DAN: Did she now?

DERRY: *(Glances at Soren)* Look, I've been trying to tell you … I've asked Soren to marry me.

VIOLET: *(Standing up)* What?

JOHN-DAN: So it's true. I knew it! *(To Soren)* Think you'll get what you came for, don't you?

SOREN: I don't know what you mean.

JOHN-DAN: *(Turning on Mary-Jo)* Did you know about this? Did you!?

MARY-JO: No!

DERRY: She didn't!

JOHN-DAN: Well it's not happening!

Suddenly a slap makes all three of them turn. Violet is standing by Soren who holds her face.

SOREN: Violet!

MARY-JO: In the name of God —

VIOLET: You think you'll go marrying out? You think— *(She shakes her violently but Soren pushes her away)* Betray your own kind — how dare you? Look at you! And your husband not clay-cold!

JOHN-DAN: Well at least we're agreed on that much Miss Grimson. There'll be no mixed marriage under my roof. From this night, I'm holding you responsible for her.

DERRY: Daddy listen—

VIOLET: Well *you'd* better be responsible for *his* behaviour.

JOHN-DAN: *(To Soren and Violet)* Now go on into the room, we can arrange things tomorrow.

DERRY: Will you listen to me for once!

SOREN: Please, John-Dan!

JOHN-DAN: Get into the room I said!

Violet grabs a lamp and ushers Soren into the parlour. Silence. Mary-Jo goes to Derry, puts her hand on his shoulder.

MARY-JO: *(Quietly)* Please, don't repulse them like this John-Dan.

JOHN-DAN: 'Tis between me and him. No one else …

MARY-JO: I'm only saying, you don't have to cut us all to bits.

JOHN-DAN: Keep outa this you. He's *my* son!

MARY-JO: I reared him didn't I? I've a right to see him happy is all I want. *(Grabs her coat)* That's all I ever wanted, not that you'd give a curse!

DERRY: Mary-Jo wait!

She bangs out the back door. Pause.

DERRY: Look ... Daddy—

JOHN-DAN: Son I know you don't mean to go making little of me.

DERRY: I want to marry Soren.

JOHN-DAN: No Protestant is going to get a holda my land. I'd sooner there wasn't a mankind on it. And every four-forked animal sold! ...

DERRY: *(Going towards him)* My mind's made up — I'm marrying her Daddy.

JOHN-DAN: Then you may go outa this! Offa my land altogether! ...

DERRY: What're you saying to me?

JOHN-DAN: There's the door, go on ...

DERRY: Leave here? How, how could I ...?

JOHN-DAN: Well if you mean to stay on under *my* roof, you may forego that woman!

John-Dan grabs the remaining lamp and exits out the stairs door. Derry stands looking after him in the glow of the Sacred Heart. He holds his head in his hands. Black out.

Scene Three

The next day, March 16th, evening. The lights come up on the kitchen where Soren is sitting by the fire. At one end of the table sits Mary-Jo pretending to do her embroidery. At the other end sits Violet, polishing a pair of boots. No one speaks as Violet watches Soren and Mary-Jo watches Violet.

MARY-JO: *(To Soren)* I know what I have left, a nice piece of salt ling. Would do you good ... Will you try it?

SOREN: Honestly, I don't want anything.

MARY-JO: *(Stopping her)* You've nothing ate since yesterday.

VIOLET: That's her own choice entirely, I wouldn't be worrying about her.

Silence. Derry comes in the back door.

MARY-JO: Well?

DERRY: Still no sign of him. Beats me altogether.

MARY-JO: Sure where could he be gone all day like this. Without saying a word.

DERRY: Haven't a clue. But I'm not going searching any more.

MARY-JO: He's never gone back up after the ewes is he?

DERRY: *(Sitting down)* I don't know where he's got to. Didn't open his mouth to me.

Pause. Violet watches Soren who goes to stand near Derry.

VIOLET: I think you might be wise to go in and lie down a while Soren.

SOREN: I lay down last night, I'm not lying down this evening.

She and Derry exchange a look. Suddenly John-Dan arrives in the back door.

MARY-JO: God's sake! Where were you? We were looking everywhere ... *(John-Dan walks past her and fills a cup of water)* Will you answer me!

JOHN-DAN: What?

MARY-JO: Where'd you disappear to?

JOHN-DAN: *(Drinks)* Nowhere.

MARY-JO: What d'you mean 'nowhere'? You musta been someplace! ...

JOHN-DAN: *(Going over to a window)* I decided to go down and see Cafferty.

Mary-Jo and Derry look at one another.

DERRY: What d'you go near him for?

MARY-JO: I thought you weren't going to be bothered?

JOHN-DAN: Well I changed my mind after. *(Soren sits down next to Derry. John-Dan turns and stops when he sees them. Pause. Violet watches him as he sits near the fire)* Did the hoggets get their feeding?

DERRY: 'Course they did — I wasn't below in Caffertys was I?

JOHN-DAN: Clean out the byre?

DERRY: Only half — spent most of the day out looking for you.

MARY-JO: You coulda told us, spared us all that worry.

Pause.

JOHN-DAN: *(To Derry)* You wouldn't mind going upstairs? Think I left my pipe up there ... *(Derry hesitates, then goes. John-Dan turns to Soren)* While you remain under my roof, I'll allow you'll sit beside your aunt.

Soren looks at him, stands, takes the brush and starts sweeping over by the back door. Silence. Mary-Jo stuffs her embroidery away. Just as Derry returns, the back door opens and Neilus enters. Violet stands as everyone stares at him.

VIOLET: Lord save us.

SOREN: Neilus!

VIOLET: How on earth—

SOREN: *(Backing away)* How did you find me?

He doesn't answer but turns to John-Dan.

NEILUS: Neilus Grimson's the name.

JOHN-DAN: So I've heard. John-Dan Lonergan. This is my sister, Mary-Jo. *(Derry looks at John-Dan in disbelief. Neilus offers his hand but Mary-Jo turns away)* And that's Derry. My son.

Derry glares at Neilus.

VIOLET: *(Going over)* How in heaven's name did you find us?

NEILUS: *(Taking off his hat and gloves)* Kept asking, didn't I. Kept on after ye.

He smiles at Soren.

SOREN: What're you smirking at me for? You're only after wasting your time!

NEILUS: Now don't be firing up your temper cousin. I'm here now. I tracked you down.

Mary-Jo looks over at John-Dan who looks away.

VIOLET: *(Taking his hands)* You're frozen with the cold. *(Giving him her scarf)* Here, rub your hands. Get the blood circulating again.

NEILUS: *(Looking at Soren)* I took out on foot after you. And walked and walked, everywhere under the moon! Been going for weeks through snow and slop and all … But I knew I'd find you sometime. Just needed a bita luck, that's all.

DERRY: Well luck doesn't folly after tyrants in this here country.

John-Dan walks over and stands beside Derry. Pause.

NEILUS: Mister Lonergan, I'm come to relieve you of your guests. They won't be needing any more of your hospitality. You're coming home Soren.

DERRY: No way in the world — she's not!

JOHN-DAN: I'm handling this Derry.

Pause.

SOREN: *(To Neilus)* You're after making a terrible mistake coming here. All that walking's been in vain.

NEILUS: You know there's only one way of resolving this. Refuse and your parents are lost … *(She looks away)* You have a duty Soren.

SOREN: To be yoked to you?

NEILUS: There's six generations reared on that land. Think of your parents. Your poor father — it's killing him.

SOREN: Let him sell half and start again.

NEILUS: Sell!

SOREN: Yes.

NEILUS: Are you raving?

SOREN: Swallow his pride!

NEILUS: The Lord man! He'd rather sell his soul!

SOREN: No, you see — he thought he could sell mine ...

NEILUS: Soren, don't be foolish—

SOREN: I'm free of that place now. When I fled it I allowed I'd never go back.

NEILUS: *(Going nearer)* Think of your child then. Marry me and I'll give the child a home where he belongs.

SOREN: You don't understand—

NEILUS: Where you both belong!

SOREN: Neilus! I've already chosen my husband.

Pasue. Neilus looks at John-Dan.

NEILUS: I see ... I was hoping we'd be able to do this civilised.

He takes a length of rope from his coat pocket.

VIOLET: You can't endanger the child Neilus!

She grabs the rope off him.

NEILUS: I'm not leaving here without her!

VIOLET: Neither am I.

SOREN: What d'you mean?

Pause.

VIOLET: Better you marry Neilus than betray your own kind.

SOREN: What!

VIOLET: Marrying out is the worst possible betrayal.

SOREN: I belong with Derry!

VIOLET: You belong with your own church, not turning your back!

MARY-JO: You're wrong Violet!

DERRY: She wouldn't have to turn her back!

MARY-JO: Crossing the gates is starting to happen here. People realise they have power over their own two feet!

VIOLET: Betrayal — that's all it is. No two ways about it! *(She turns to Neilus)* I'll tell you now what we'll do.

NEILUS: What?

VIOLET: You'll go back into Tinahely and get some sort of a sleigh put together. Come back here tomorrow and bring some men to help you pull it. *(To Soren)* We're all three of us leaving here together.

DERRY: *(To John-Dan)* Do you not hear what she's after saying? Daddy!

JOHN-DAN: This marriage is not going ahead.

DERRY: *(Suddenly going for Neilus)* You'll never take her from me!

Derry hits Neilus who fights back, but John-Dan restrains Derry and Mary-Jo intervenes.

MARY-JO: Derry don't!

JOHN-DAN: I want no fighting!

MARY-JO: Not like this! Don't leave yourself down, d'you hear me?

NEILUS: I'll go — before I really let my temper loose. I wasn't warned I'd be met with violence!

He exits. Mary-Jo stares after him. Pause.

SOREN: *(To Violet)* I thought I understood you Violet

VIOLET: Well now you know better, don't you?

Silence. Rain begins to fall lightly.

MARY-JO: What's he after saying there? Said he wasn't warned, 'bout violence. *(She looks at John-Dan who goes over to the fire)* 'Twas you brought him here, didn't you?

JOHN-DAN: Mary-Jo don't be—

MARY-JO: That's where you were the whole of the day. Never went near Cafferty!

JOHN-DAN: It's my land and I will protect it.

MARY-JO: Only minding the land, you were only ever minding it!

Derry goes over and stands looking at John-Dan.

JOHN-DAN: Land is a terrible responsibility Derry.

DERRY: That's all you have to say to me is it?

JOHN-DAN: You're young, your heart'll easy recover. The land is a different thing.

Derry looks at him and turns away.

VIOLET: Soren — come on inside.

SOREN: No.

VIOLET: Get in there now — I'm warning you!

JOHN-DAN: *(To Soren)* There'll be no more discussing! *(To Derry)* This night's come to an end.

MARY-JO: *(To John-Dan)* Can't you allow them a parting moment alone. Can't you grant them that much?

JOHN-DAN: *(Shrugs)* What harm.

He exits out the stairs door.

VIOLET: *(To Soren)* A minute then. But no more.

Violet exits into the parlour.

MARY-JO: He'll live to regret this rashness ... They both will. I know it.

She exits out the stairs door. Pause. The rain gets heavier.

DERRY: So that's all means anything to him. Land before all else! He'd rather bury us beneath it. Pull our hearts to bits!

SOREN: What can we do? Is there nothing we can do!

DERRY: *(Turning to her)* I'd go outa this — I would! But the snow has us trapped. We're caught!

He hugs her. After a moment, Soren looks up and whispers.

SOREN: Derry ... Listen ...

The rain pours down. Black out.

Scene Four

Saint Patrick's Day. Early morning. Offstage the boys whoop and cheer.

PASCAL: *(Offstage)* Hi! Lonergans!

MIXIE: *(Offstage)* Are ye in there?

PASCAL: *(Offstage)* Hello!

MIXIE: *(Offstage)* Anybody home?

They come tearing in the back door and stop dead.

MIXIE: Nobody up, they mustn't realise! Call them you Pascal!

PASCAL: Derry! John-Dan? … Mary-Jo, are you awake?

MIXIE: That's strange isn't it?

PASCAL: *(Roaring)* C'mon — are ye alive or dead or what!

MIXIE: *(Boxing him)* Jay Pascal stop — there'll be slaughter!

PASCAL: *(Threatening him)* Don't mind hitting me!

Mary-Jo opens the stairs door. She looks exhausted.

MARY-JO: Whist up! The shouts of ye!

Pascal grabs her and twirls her around.

PASCAL: Mary-Jo, it's a miracle!

MIXIE: It's true!

MARY-JO: Leave go! Stop it!

She pushes him away.

PASCAL: Don't say you didn't hear the floodsa rain last night?

MIXIE: A sea of water, lashing outa the heavens!

MARY-JO: Rain? Aye, what about it!

PASCAL: It's Saint Patrick. He's after working a miracle!

MIXIE: You won't believe it.

PASCAL: Look! *(Bringing her over to a window)* Patrick's after bringing the thaw.

MARY-JO: Sacred.

All three look out.

MIXIE: There now, isn't that the greenest green you ever saw in your life!

MARY-JO: So it's come, at long last …

PASCAL: I tell you that colour's some sight to behold, after weeks and weeks of whiteness …

Mary-Jo puts her hand to her face.

MIXIE: Are you alright?

PASCAL: She wasn't expecting it — were you? *(Mary-Jo shakes her head)* Well you might look a bit more happy 'bout it!

Mixie makes a face at him.

MIXIE: Mary-Jo what's wrong?

MARY-JO: *(Turning away)* Oh, nothing … *(The boys watch her walk away)* Mixie, will you go up and get Derry down to see it. I haven't the heart to go calling him myself.

MIXIE: 'Course I will. You sit yourself down.

Mixie exits upstairs. Mary-Jo stands looking out the other window.

PASCAL: I'll go on out to the stable, turn the poor horses loose! They won't know themselves — isn't it great?

MARY-JO: Yeh, powerful. *(Pascal exits outside. Pause. Mary-Jo sees Derry's handkerchief on the ground. She goes over and picks it up, smiles. Slowly she folds it as Violet enters from the parlour)*

VIOLET: *(Pulling on her cardigan)* Is it true? *(Mary-Jo looks at her)* About the thaw — is it true?

MARY-JO: See for yourself.

Violet goes to a window. Mary-Jo stands watching her.

VIOLET: Oh look at that! The green of it. At last — thank the Lord.

Violet turns to speak to Mary-Jo but hesitates when she meets her gaze.

MARY-JO: Seems Saint Patrick's after doing you a favour. Won't be needing the sleigh after all.

Violet moves over near the fire. Pause.

VIOLET: Soren's gone outside is she? Didn't hear her getting up.

MARY-JO: Slept that peaceful did you? My God.

They look at one another. Mixie returns.

MIXIE: Derry's not up there.

MARY-JO: He's not?

MIXIE: Must be gone out.

Mary-Jo looks down at the handkerchief and looks back at Mixie. Pause.

VIOLET: *(Eyeing them)* What?

MIXIE: I'd say he's just, gone doing the milking ...

VIOLET: Did Soren go outside as well? ... Mary-Jo I'm talking to you, I asked you a question—

MARY-JO: How would I know, amn't I only just up myself ...?

VIOLET: I want to know where Soren is. Answer me!

MARY-JO: I haven't seen her, I'm telling you.

VIOLET: Well she did come to bed. She has to be here somewhere.

MARY-JO: *(Going towards her)* Search the place then — if you think we're hiding her. Go on, no one's stopping you!

John-Dan enters, buttoning his shirt. Violet looks at him, hesitates.

VIOLET: Right, I will.

She exits upstairs. Mixie comes over to Mary-Jo.

JOHN-DAN: *(Looking out a window)* Doesn't that beat all. Well thanks be to God. Now we'll get the planting done. Get the work going in the fields. *(To Mixie)* Where's Derry got to?

MIXIE: *(Glances at Mary-Jo)* Don't know sir.

JOHN-DAN: What're you standing there gawking! Go and find him. Tell him I want him, straight away!

Mixie doesn't move.

MARY-JO: There'll be no ploughing done John-Dan. Or you'll be doing it all alone.

JOHN-DAN: What kinda talk is that! What d'you mean?

MARY-JO: They're gone. The two of them.

JOHN-DAN: What?

Violet returns and glares at them.

VIOLET: I'm warning all of you, if Soren isn't found when those men come there'll be trouble!

JOHN-DAN: What the hell's goin' on?

MARY-JO: You're too late Violet! Thanks be to God …

PASCAL: *(Offstage)* Mary-Jo!

Pascal comes in the back door. Everyone turns to look at him.

PASCAL: Mary-Jo the horses are took! I swear, there's no sign of 'em.

JOHN-DAN: Derry … *(Rushing out the back door)* Derry!

Pause.

MARY-JO: And what about the car?

PASCAL: Gone as well.

MARY-JO: Are you sure? You checked all 'round?

PASCAL: There's nothin' out there. 'Tis empty …

Mary-Jo nods. Pascal looks at Mixie. Pause.

VIOLET: Oh dear Lord. *(Holding on to the table, she sits)* Soren …

John-Dan comes slowly in the back door and looks at the others.

JOHN-DAN: *(Shaking his head)* But, he couldn't go. He told me himself … Told me himself he'd never leave.

He slumps into a chair and holds his head in his hands. Mary-Jo walks over to a window and looks out.

MARY-JO: They're gone from us alright. Delivered from this place. And the snow, melting in their wake.

Lights fade slowly to black.

The End